# Pope Alexander VI and his court: extracts from the Latin diary of Johannes Burchardus;

Johann Burchard, F L. Glaser

# POPE ALEXANDER VI
## AND HIS COURT

# HISTORICAL MINIATURES
## A SERIES OF MONOGRAPHS
### *Edited by Dr. F. L. Glaser*

**VOL. I — SCENES FROM THE COURT OF PETER THE GREAT**

Based on the Latin Diary of John G. Korb, a secretary of the Austrian Legation at the Court of Peter the Great.

**VOL. II — POPE ALEXANDER VI AND HIS COURT**

Based on the Diary of Johannes Burchardus, Master of Ceremonies to Pope Alexander VI.

**VOL. III — LIFE IN PARIS UNDER LOUIS XV**

Extracts from the Diary of Siméon Prosper Hardy, publisher and bookseller.

# POPE ALEXANDER VI
## AND HIS COURT

EXTRACTS FROM THE LATIN DIARY OF

## JOHANNES BURCHARDUS
### BISHOP OF ORTA AND CIVITA CASTELLANA,
### PONTIFICAL MASTER OF CEREMONIES

EDITED BY
### DR. F. L. GLASER

## NICHOLAS L. BROWN
### NEW YORK    MCMXXI

A731138

# CONTENTS

| CHAPTER | | PAGE |
|---|---|---|
| | Intruduction | v |
| I | Death and Funeral of Sixtus IV | 1 |
| II | The Conclave Which Chose Innocent VIII | 11 |
| III | First Years of the Reign of Innocent VIII | 19 |
| IV | Last Years of Innocent VIII | 35 |
| V | Accession of Alexander VI | 53 |
| VI | Coronation of the King of Naples | 67 |
| VII | King Charles VIII in Rome | 77 |
| VIII | Alexander and His Family | 85 |
| IX | Life in Rome Under the Borgias | 95 |
| X | The Aggrandizement of the Borgias | 105 |
| XI | The Year of the Jubilee | 119 |
| XII | Feasts and Feuds in Rome | 143 |
| XIII | Closing Years of Alexander's Reign | 157 |
| XIV | Death and Funeral of Alexander | 179 |
| | Appendix | 189 |

# INTRODUCTION

"My dear Son:— We have learned that your Worthiness, forgetful of the high office with which you are invested, was present from the seventeenth to the twenty-second hour, four days ago, in the Gardens of John de Bichis, where there were several women of Siena, women wholly given over to worldly vanities. Your companion was one of your colleagues whom his years, if not the dignity of his office, ought to have reminded of his duty. We have heard that the dance was indulged in, in all wantonness. None of the allurements of love were lacking, and you conducted yourself in a wholly worldly manner. Shame forbids mention of all that took place, for not only the things themselves but their very names are unworthy of your rank. In order that your lust might be all the more unrestrained, the husbands, fathers, brothers and kinsmen of the young women and girls were not invited to be present. You and a few servants were the leaders and inspirers of this orgy. It is said that nothing is now talked of in Siena but your vanity which is the subject of universal ridicule. Certain it is that here at the baths, where churchmen and the laity are very numerous, your name is on every one's tongue."

The words are taken from an admonitory letter of Pope Pius II to Cardinal Rodrigo Borgia — better known to the world as Pope Alexander VI — written in June, 1460, when the young cardinal had not yet reached the thirties, and reproving him for having arranged a bacchanalian feast in Siena. No words could better characterize the personality of Alexander VI, for they show him as the man of the world he was as Cardinal Borgia and remained after he had become Pope Alexander.

The limelight of history has played in a rather oblique and unkind way on the Borgias. Pope Alexander's personality has been distorted until he became a perfect monster; yet his greatest weakness was an easy freedom from moral scruples, and this might not have blurred his personal charm at all had he not become the tool of his son Cesare. More unjust still were most historians to his daughter Lucretia, who has been depicted as a kind of Messalina, although she was at the best the "indifferente" among the great women of her time, and at her worst a beauty without any will of her own. If it is the historian's task to distribute praise and blame, some of the latter may fall on Alexander's favorite son Cesare. Even if he was not such a perfect virtuoso of crime as he has been described, he certainly was not much better than some of the worst of his more prominent contemporaries.

Thus in considering the rise and fall of the Borgia

family one ought to keep in mind that the Borgias were after all the creatures of an epoch, rich in extraordinary personalities as few others in human history have been. Before rendering judgment consideration must be given to the remarkably complex personalities of the Renaissance. The men and women of that epoch of transformation from the middle ages to modern times were so constituted that it was easily possible for them to turn from cruelty and crime and vice, from corruption and treachery, to religion with a fervid and impassioned sincerity. The Borgias, as will be seen, did not differ greatly from many of their contemporaries. To make them the scapegoats of their times shows, perhaps, a just indignation at their crimes, but little understanding of the conditions under which they lived.

Bearing in mind these conditions and the remarkable rise of the House of Borgia, one will be better prepared to understand the personality of Pope Alexander who with all his faults was certainly not without redeeming features. "Of his ability, of his genius even," says Bishop A. H. Mathew, one of his recent biographers, "there can be no two opinions; indeed if vigor of body and mind were all that was required of a pope, Alexander VI would have been among the greatest. He had a remarkable capacity for hard mental work, and his buoyant, jovial nature enabled him to bear his burden of vice and crime with a lightness impossible to a man of a less sanguine disposition." Such was the complex personality of this typical man of the Renaissance.

A fair estimate of Alexander VI must include in addition to his personal gifts and the complexities of his character a consideration of the remarkable rise of his family. It was from this source that he received a further impetus toward that most seductive of all human temptations — the abuse of power. The Borgias like the Bonapartes three centuries later in France were neither an old nor a native family. They had come from Spain where their ancestors had participated in the expulsion of the Moors in the thirteenth century, their family name being derived from their native place of Borjia on the borders of Aragon, Castile and Navarre.

But with the election of one of their family, Alonzo Borgia, as Pope Calixtus III, in the middle of the fifteenth century, they became prominent in the affairs of the European world just at the moment when Italy, then the most advanced country of that continent, had cast off the fetters of mediæval envelopment and entered upon the most brilliant period of its cultural development. Calixtus III had been a professor of jurisprudence in Lerida in Spain, where he won the reputation of being one of the foremost jurists of his time. He had come to Rome as a legal adviser to King Alphonso of Naples. His knowledge and character and his extreme age which made it certain that he would not be long in the way of other aspirants to the papal tiara finally secured his elevation to the highest place in Christendom.

In contrast to the other papal elections of the time the nomination of Calixtus III was not accompanied by the sneering remarks which such occasions usually called forth. Although his reign lasted only three years he managed to secure a firm footing for the Borgia family in the Roman hierarchy. He may indeed be considered as one of the initiators of nepotism in the papacy, and the first ruler of the Roman church, who founded a kind of family dynasty through the promotion of his nephews. Two of these, Luis and Rodrigo Borgia (later Pope Alexander VI) became cardinals, while a third who was not a priest was promoted to the captaincy-general of the papal state and created duke of Spoleto. The latter, as prefect of Rome, had also to keep in check the old families of the Colonna and Orsini, the traditional enemies of the papal rule in the Holy City.

While Calixtus III kept on the defensive against his enemies in the city of his residence, he followed the papal tradition of crusading against the Turk. The latter had just taken possession of Constantinople and made it his capital. The power of the Turkish empire was spreading in South-Eastern Europe, and to war against it Calixtus brought great sacrifices, selling the jewels of the papal treasury and other possessions of the Church. For another and greater phenomenon of his time, the Renaissance in Italy, Pope Calixtus had no understanding. The humanists complained that he never gave them a helping hand, and that he even sold the precious golden bindings of Greek manuscripts in order to finance his expeditions against the Turks.

The successors of Calixtus III held other views. Literature and the arts flourished under their patronage. Painters and sculptors, writers and savants, thronged the papal Court. This intrusion of scantily disguised agnosticism into the heart of the church frightened the pious and the conservatives who heard the first rumblings of the Reformation. Paul II restored the pagan monuments of Rome, and, after the Medici of Florence, was the greatest collector of the time. The successor of Paul, Sixtus IV, went even further. The principal result of his reign was the secularization of the papacy. For Sixtus IV was a worldly prince in the full sense of the word. The aim of his policy was not even the extension of the power of the Holy See, but primarily the enrichment of his relatives and favorites. With his approval the Medici were murdered by the Pazzi family, a design which could not be accomplished completely and which finally reacted to the disadvantage of the Pope himself. There was an increasing demand for a council which should depose this ruler of the church " without religion and con-

science who was called the Pope "; a pious poet of
the time wailed over the fact that everything was at
sale in Rome: "Temples, priests, altars and even
prayers, heaven and God." In August, 1484, Sixtus
died, at the age of seventy, a martyr to gout and
worn out with rage at the news of the peace which
had been made between the Duke of Ferrara and the
Venetians without his consent.

In the eyes of the critics of the Holy See the reign
of Innocent VIII (1484–1492) was no improve-
ment. He was the first Pope who dared to acknowl-
edge his son in public, and one of his chief aims
was to procure him wealth and position. If Sixtus
had secured money through the sale of spiritual
indulgences and dignities, Innocent and his son obtained it through a bank of secular pardons where
amnesty for murder could be had at high fees. A
hundred and fifty ducats of every fine went to the
papal treasury, the rest to the Pope's son, Frances-
chetto Cibo. Special traps were set in Rome to
catch the criminals who were able to pay the Pope
for their misdeeds. In the meantime Innocent
looked on complacently from his well-guarded palace
at the increasing criminality in Rome. This Fran-
ceschetto had only one aim in life, and this was to
get the papal treasure-chests in his hands as soon
as his father died. When in 1490 a false rumor
spread that the Pope had died, he attempted in fact
to carry off all the available cash of the papal

Camera. He even tried to take along the Turkish Prince Zizim who lived as a prisoner at the papal court, hoping to sell him at a high price to one of the many foreign rulers who were anxious to get possession of him.

Rodrigo Borgia, who succeeded Innocent VIII two years after this incident, was born at Xativa, Spain, in 1431, and became a priest in 1468. The man of the world, who was so admired in his later life, was foreshadowed in the boy, for at the age of scarcely eight years he was conspicuous in the streets of his home town for the grace and gallantry of his bearing. After having been educated at Valencia, he studied at the University of Bologna, and on his return to Spain he practiced successfully as an advocate. In 1456 Calixtus III bestowed the cardinal's purple upon his nephew, and a year later the important office of vice-chancellor of the Church of Rome was conferred on him.

By the historian Gasparino of Verona the young Cardinal is thus described: "He is handsome; of a most glad countenance and joyous aspect, gifted with honeyed and choice eloquence. The beautiful women on whom his eyes are cast he lures to love him, and moves them in a wondrous way, more powerfully than the magnet influences iron." It appears, however, that only three women played a prominent rôle in his life. The first was Vanozza dei Catanei, and in his later life the beautiful Giulia

Farnese is openly mentioned as his mistress. In the intervening period his niece, Hadriana Orsini, seems to have had relations with him, but she patiently effaced herself when any other intimate acquaintance of Alexander was concerned. He never forgot Vanozza, whom he had met in his earlier life; she was born in 1442 and died in 1518, and was the mother of his dearest children. She always lived in magnificence, and enjoyed the possession of the various palaces which her lover had given her.

At the time when he was still practicing law Rodrigo Borgia made the acquaintance of a widow and her two daughters. He entered into intimate relations with the mother, and after her death became guardian of the girls. One of these he sent to a convent; the other he made his mistress. This was Vanozza, who is described by contemporaries as a combination of voluptuous beauty, amiability, and shrewdness. He had five children by her, but he did not recognize them openly until after he became Pope. The oldest was Pedro Luis, first Duke of Gandia, who was born about 1467; Giovanni was born in 1474 and assassinated 1498 (see p. 89), and Cesare in 1476. The other two children were Donna Lucretia, born in 1480, and Don Jofré, born in 1481. About 1480 Cardinal Borgia in order to cover up his relations with Vanozza and to lighten his own burden found a husband for her. He obtained a position as apostolic secretary for him from

Pope Sixtus IV. This is the only marriage mentioned.

None of Vanozza's contemporaries have given any clue as to the gifts that enabled her to hold the pleasure-loving cardinal so securely and to obtain for her recognition as the mother of several of his acknowledged children. She was of Roman origin and came from a middle-class family. "We may imagine her," says the historian Gregorovius, "to have been a strong and voluptuous woman like those still seen about the streets of Rome. They possess none of the grace of the ideal woman of the Umbrian school, but they have something of the magnificence of the imperial city — Juno and Venus are united in them. They would resemble the ideals of Titian and Paolo Veronese but for their black hair and dark complexion,— blond and red hair have always been rare among the Romans. But without doubt Vanozza was of great beauty and ardent passions; for if not, how could she have maintained her relations with the cardinal?"

Rodrigo Borgia secured his accession to the Holy See by buying the necessary majority through promises and bribery. A short while before the meeting of the Conclave, for instance, he had sent four mule-loads of silver to Cardinal Sforza's house on the pretext that it might be more safely guarded there. After his election in 1492 he hurried on the same night to St. Peter's for the inaugural ceremonies. A contemporary, Sigismondo de' Conti, said of the new Pope: " Few people understand etiquette so well as he did; he knew how to make most of himself, and took pains to shine in conversation and to be dignified in his manners. In the latter point his majestic stature gave him an advantage. Also he was just at the age (about sixty) at which Aristotle says that men are wisest. Robust in body and vigorous in mind, he was admirably well equipped for his new position. He was tall and powerfully built, and, though his eyes were blinking, they were penetrating and lively; in conversation he was extremely affable; he understood money matters thoroughly." Another contemporary, Hieronymus Portius, describing him in 1493, says: " Alexander is tall and neither light nor dark, his eyes are black and his lips somewhat full. His health is robust, and he is able to bear any pain or fatigue. He is wonderfully eloquent and a thorough man of the world." The celebrated Jason Mainus of Milan calls attention to his elegance of figure, his serene brow, his kingly forehead, his countenance with its expression of generosity and majesty, his genius, and the heroic beauty of his whole presence.

It was a happy combination of mind and body, and its power lay in the perfect balance of all its faculties. It was a personality which radiated serene brightness, for the picture often drawn of this Borgia, as a sinister monster, is not true to life.

Quite on the contrary, and unlike his son Cesare, says Bishop A. H. Mathew in his biography of Rodrigo Borgia, Alexander does not appear to have been wantonly inhuman although the prevalent belief that he poisoned [1] his cardinals when his treasury needed replenishing can neither be proved nor disproved (see p. 178). But he did not revel in cruelty as cruelty though he certainly never let any humane scruples stand in the way of his own advancement. He was not a tyrant in the ordinary sense of the word, being preserved from that vice as a rule by his natural geniality.

The advancement of his family became, as the years of his reign went on, more and more the dominant passion of Alexander, but at the same time the organization of the Roman Curia was improved and the salaries of officials were paid punctually. The latter had not always been a custom under former Popes. The administration of justice in Rome and the Papal State was also made more effective, and in time of famine the poor were helped with supplies of corn from Sicily. " Nevertheless," admits Mathew, " the populace detested their Pope with a deadly loathing, and the fact that Rodrigo Borgia was permitted to occupy the throne of St. Peter for a

[1] The famous slow and effective white powder used by the Borgias was arsenic, and they probably used it more successfully and perhaps more frequently than others of that period.

space of ten years affords remarkable proof of the strength of the later mediæval Papacy."

In every day life Alexander VI is described of being genial and pleasant and fond of talking, so much so that he was almost incapable of keeping a secret. He was impetuous, but he rarely bore malice, and he had but little sympathy with the vindictive spirit constantly displayed by his son Cesare. Naturally unreserved and expansive, he never hid his joy at the success of his schemes. To inferiors he showed himself affable, and it is said that he " liked to do unpleasant things in a pleasant manner." Although religious formalities meant nothing to him, he was much concerned in ceremonies when they served his purpose. But to the rules of Lenten abstinence he paid little regard and at the solemn mass sung on the arrival in Rome of King Charles VIII of France he confused all the ceremonies. Nevertheless he cherished a particular devotion for the Blessed Virgin and in her honor he revived the custom of ringing the bells during the recantation of the Angelus thrice a day. One of his greatest delights was to watch beautiful women dancing. When Lucretia and the ladies of her court were engaged in this art, he was careful to summon the ambassadors of Ferrara so that they might watch his daughter's grace, for he was anxious to see her married to the son of the duke.

This plan he achieved in the year 1501 when Lucretia was married to Alphonso d'Este. After this marriage and until her death in 1519 Lucretia seems to have lived a comparatively quiet and happy life. During her earlier life she was much maligned and accused of many crimes; as a matter of fact, she was always the tool of her father and brother. In 1493, at the age of thirteen years, she had been married to Giovanni Sforza, and a gorgeous banquet was given to celebrate the event. After spending a happy and careless year at her husband's beautiful estate of Pesaro, her marriage took a bad turn because the house of Sforza was fast losing its former prestige. Giovanni's life was threatened if he did not give up the Pope's daughter. In 1497 the final divorce was pronounced. Lucretia's attitude in the whole affair became the subject of much satire and criticism. But in the following year she entered into a second marriage with Alphonso Bisceglia, a natural son of King Alphonso II of Naples. Her husband was considered "one of the most beautiful men of Italy," and was seven years younger than she. Threatened by the open hatred of Cesare Borgia, Alphonso flew from Rome during the following year, but returned a few months later with Lucretia, who was passionately enamored of her handsome husband. In the summer of 1500 Alphonso was wounded mortally by assassins who probably acted under orders of the Orsini family. Alphonso considered Cesare as the real instigator of the assault, and shot at him as he left his house after calling on him and was cut to pieces by Cesare's guards.

Lucretia was only a tool of the Borgias, father and son, but Cesare was the pride and center of the family. From 1497 on he was the real ruler of the Pontifical State, and Alexander frequently seems to have submitted to his will against his own better judgment. The crown of Italy was Cesare's ambition. The plottings of the Pope with the Kings of France and Naples and other Italian rulers had their origin in this wish, which burned more violently in the breast of this gifted and demonic son of Alexander than in that of other Italian tyrants of the time. Working toward this end the Borgias decided upon the annihilation of the prominent Italian families. The Gaetani and the Orsini were thus exterminated (see p. 171); the Colonnas and others were driven from their possessions. In the midst of this slaughter and assassination stood Cesare, and Alexander put all the money and influence of the church at his disposal.

Pope Sixtus IV already had favored young Cesare. Scarcely seven years old he received from him the income of the Cathedral of Valencia, two years later he was made provost of Abar; at the age of fifteen Innocent VIII created him Bishop of Pamplona. After the coronation of his father he became Archbishop of Valencia and a few years later a cardinal.

From the bishopric of Valencia Cesare drew an annual income of 16,000 ducats. But even under the then existing conditions he found priesthood too great an obstacle for his political ambitions, and he resigned the cardinalate to devote himself to his military and political plans.

Before his excesses and the disease resulting from them disfigured him and forced him occasionally to wear a mask, he possessed great beauty and strength. He could cut off a bull's head with one stroke, he bent an iron bar and broke a horseshoe with his hands, and he tore a new rope. His strong body was graceful, and he was admired as an accomplished dancer and horseman. He loved precious clothes and rare weapons which are described at length in the diplomatic reports of the time; his sword was known as the king of swords. He remained always a Spaniard, preferring the Spanish tongue and preserving the proud senstitiveness of a Spanish grandee even in respect to the written word touching his personality. The more jovial personality of Alexander permitted a remarkable freedom of expression, but Cesare persecuted all criticism directed against him with savage cruelty. When Alexander remarked that Rome was a free city where every one could write and say what he pleased, Cesare replied that he would make repent those who did so. If he succeeded in seizing one who had written a Pasquinade against him he had his tongue sliced with a red-hot dagger and both his hands cut off. He frequently indulged in needless cruelty. One day he had six men brought in the street before St. Peter's, and they were hunted like game with crossbows in the closed street. Many murders were ascribed to him by his contemporaries; a few of these have been proven to have been the deeds of others. Thus he was held responsible for the murder of his brother, Cardinal Giovanni Borgia, but it is more likely that this mysterious assassination was an act of revenge on the part of an offended husband.

On account of his magnificent physique Cesare attracted women, but they played a much smaller rôle in his life than many of the sensational biographies would have us believe. Only one real love adventure is reported, and that was during the winter of 1500 when he had his Spanish horsemen seize the wife of one of the captains of the Republic of Venice. The Republic sent a formal protest to Pope Alexander, who regretted the incident. But no word of protest was heard from Dorotea, the abducted wife, who a few years later wrote to the Republic of San Marco that she was willing to return to her husband in case good treatment would be assured her. There is also mentioned a strong and beautiful woman companion during one of his campaigns. Women may have been a certain distraction in his hours of leisure, but they meant little in his life. His marriage with Charlotte d'Albret, a sister of the King of Navarre, had lasted scarcely four months, when Cesare returned to Rome. He never saw his wife again nor did he ever see his daughter Louise born in 1500. His style of life was considered peculiar even in that time for he seldom rose before three o'clock in the afternoon and went to bed at the twilight of the morning.

After the death of Pope Alexander the star of Cesare declined. A few weeks after Cardinal Giuliano Rovere had become Pope Julius II, Cesare was arrested and taken to Rome. He was set at liberty soon afterward, however, without the knowledge of the Pope and escaped to Naples, where he was seized again and sent to Spain. There he was kept under strict confinement in various castles, and his only recreation was flying his falcons and watching them as they seized upon their prey and tore it to pieces. In 1506 he again escaped and fell in battle the same year as the commander of an army of his brother-in-law, the King of Navarre.

Thus ended the Borgias, father and son. Their graves are unknown. Their crimes have been exaggerated, but the works of artists they encouraged and patronized are still extant. Raphael, Michelangelo, and Pinturicchio worked for the Borgias, and Copernicus lectured in Rome during the year of the jubilee on his new theory of the motion of the heavenly bodies. If this Pope has been called the most charactertistic incarnation of the secular spirit in the papacy of the fifteenth century, it should be remem-

bered that the secularization of the papacy had be-
gun with Sixtus IV and that it was as conspicuous
under Innocent VIII as under Alexander VI.

---

The minute descriptions in Burchard's Diary help
us to understand the contradictory elements in the
many-sided character of Alexander VI, and show it
in its relations with politics, war, government, love,
and religion. Of the description of Alexander's
court in this Diary, Gregorovius, one of the foremost authorities of the period, says: " Never did
any chronicler describe the things about him so
clearly and so concisely, so dryly, and with so little
feeling — things that were worthy of the pen of
Tacitus. That Burchard was not friendly to the
Borgias is proved by the way his diary is written.
It is, however, absolutely truthful. This man well
knew how to conceal his feelings, if the dull routine
of his office had left him any. He went through
the daily ceremonies of the Vatican mechanically and
kept his place there under five popes. Burchard
must have appeared to the Borgias as a harmless
pedant; for if not, would they have permitted him to
behold and describe their doings and yet live? Even
the little he did write in his Diary concerning events
of the day would have cost him his head had it come
to the knowledge of Alexander or Cesare. It appears, however, that the diaries of the masters of
ceremonies were not subjected to official censorship.

Cesare would have spared him no more than he did his father's favorite, Pedro Calderon Perotto, whom he stabbed, and Cervillon (se p. 117), whom he killed — both of whom frequently performed important parts in the ceremonies of the Vatican. Nor did Cesare spare the private secretary, Francesco Troche, whom Alexander VI had often employed in diplomatic affairs. There is no doubt that he was one of Lucretia's most intimate acquaintances. In June, 1503, Cesare had this favorite of his father strangled." This fate would have awaited the author of the present Diary had its existence ever come to the knowledge of the Borgias. Johannes Burchardus (or Burchard) was born near Strasburg, in Alsace, in the middle of the fifteen century. Destined for the Church, he was educated from his earliest childhood in an ecclesiastical environment. Instead of following a course of theology which then required ten years' close study to obtain the Doctor's degree, Burchard, practical man that he was, chose an easier way, that of the law, where the course of study was only four years, and the hope of honor and fortune equally sure. Four years after having received his Doctor's cap he indeed succeeded with the help of friends in reaching Rome. Here advocates found a lucrative income in the numberless lawsuits that were incessantly before the ecclesiastical courts. The pursuit of benefices, characteristic of the time, gave rise to numerous acts of injustice, and owners turned out of their rightful possessions did not give them up without a protest.

Opportunity soon knocked at the door of the young lawyer at the Papal court. Agostino Patrizzi, assistant master of ceremonies and a friend of Burchard, longed to retire. Supported by Patrizzi's recommendation it was an easy matter for Burchard to secure the appointment, and in December, 1483, he was installed as a Clerk of the Ceremonies. As soon as he entered upon his office, Burchard resolved to note down all details relating to his duties, so as to have a guide for precedents of conduct. At first he confined himself to entering notes of little general interest. Later, seeing how much advantage there was in fuller accounts, he expanded his notes. The Diary really begins with the death of Sixtus IV, in August, 1484, and a striking account is given how the Pope was left dead and naked upon a table, while the officials and servants of his palace were carrying off everything upon which they could lay their hands.

Innocent VIII, his successor, was at once besieged with petitions from the cardinals who had given him their votes. He signed everything without question, and in the wholesale distribution of grants and favors Burchard took care that he was not overlooked. Although a sceptic with regard to everything outside his own office, Burchard showed all the passion of a pedant in his observance of the ceremonial for which he was responsible. Lapses of eti-

quette caused him acute annoyance. But it is just
this pedantry which makes his diary especially valuable. It is just the lymphatic, egotistic, unimagina-
tive qualities in a man like Burchard that give his
detailed narrative the stamp of truth, and there is
little doubt that he is one of the most trustworthy
contemporary witnesses.

This is especially true of the outside dealing with
the court of Alexander VI, for during this period
he devotes increasing attention to political incidents
and anecdotal sidelights. The part of the Diary covering the reign of Innocent VIII has, of course, an
interest and value for the special student of history,
but it would scarcely have rescued the author's name
from obscurity.

The Diary not only gives an account of many of
the important political events of the reign of Alexander, but also glimpses into the intimate daily life.
There is the story of the supper which Cesare Borgia
gave to fifty courtesans in his apartments at the
Vatican in the presence of the Pope himself and his
sister Lucretia. That this banquet actually took
place cannot be doubted, for the Florentine orator,
Capello, wrote a few days after the feast to the
Seignory: " The Pope has not been to St. Peter's of
late, for the feast of All Saints, nor for All Souls,
nor the chapel. They say that he has taken cold,
but that fact did not hinder him on Sunday evening,

All Saints Eve, from sitting up until midnight with the Duke, who had invited courtesans and public women to the Vatican. They spent the night in dancing and rioting."

Pius III had made Burchard Bishop of Orta and Civita Castellana, and other honors and offices were conferred on him under Julius II. But his health began to fail and the entries in the Diary became more condensed. On November 16th, 1505, he witnessed the marriage of Laura Orsini, the daughter of Giulia Farnese and Pope Alexander, with Nicholas della Rovere, nephew to Pope Julius II. " The adulterous wife," says Paris de Grassis, a colleague of Burchard, " the mistress of Pope Alexander VI, the butt of all the satirists of Rome and Italy, now entered the Vatican as the most distinguished woman in the Roman aristocracy, for the purpose of uniting her daughter with the Pope's nephew. The late Pope seemed thereby absolved from all his crimes."

In March, 1506, Burchard went to Viterbo to take the waters, where the famous spring of Bulicame attracted the fashionable society of the neighborhood and the great prelates of the Roman Court. It was, moreover the resort of the demimonde of Rome, the " honest courtesans," as Burchard calls them in his Diary. His office soon called him again and he superintended the ceremony of laying the foundation stone of the Basilica of St. Peter, and in May, 1506, he died. "His end was melancholy" was the comment of a friend who added a few lines to the Diary whose last entry was made on April 27th, 1506.

This Diary remains, as Bishop A. H. Mathew points out, the most valuable record we possess of the history of the Popes at the end of the fifteenth century and the beginning of the sixteenth. The historians of the sixteenth, seventeenth and eighteenth centuries used it as the main source of their information, but up to the second half of the nineteenth century only extracts of the Diary, from manuscripts in various libraries, were published. One of these extracts was brought out in 1696 by the philosopher Leibnitz under the title: *Specimen Historiae Arcanae, sive anecdota de vita Alexandri VI Papae.* In 1854 Achille Gennarelli published in Florence an account of the pontificate of Innocent VIII and the first two years of that of Alexander VI. But the obstacles placed in his way by the government of the Grand Duke of Tuscany and the annoyances to which he was subjected, forced him to abandon the publication of the Diary, which had been copied as far as May 15th, 1494.

In the years 1883–1885 L. Thuasne brought out in Paris the first complete Latin edition of Burchard's Diary in three volumes, based on the manuscripts in the libraries of Paris, Rome and Florence. This edition was used in part for the English translation of Burchard's Diary by Bishop A. H. Mathew of which, however, only the first volume, covering the years 1483–1492, has appeared (London, 1910). But even this translation is not absolutely complete, for in order to make the work not too cumbersome, minor details, such as long lists of names, or weights and sizes of wax candles or repetitions in documents and the like, were omitted.

In the present volume the omissions had to be made on a much larger scale, and all unessentials had to be eliminated.  To give as comprehensive a picture of the times as possible some of Burchard's entries during the reigns of Sixtus IV and Innocent VIII have been included, and in these use has been made of Bishop A. H. Mathew's translation.

The editor's aim throughout has been to make available to a larger public the treasures hidden away in the endless details of the diary, and he hopes that in the passages selected he has succeeded in conveying to the reader the characteristic features of a remarkable period and its complex personalities as recorded by a contemporary.

F. L. GLASER.

New York, March, 1921.

# POPE ALEXANDER VI
# AND HIS COURT

## I

## THE DEATH AND FUNERAL OF POPE SIXTUS IV

SEEING that it behooves a Master of the Ceremonies to pay heed to individuals, I, John Burchard, Clerk of the Ceremonies in the chapel of His Holiness our Lord the Pope, will note below the things which happened in my time and appeared to be connected with ceremonies, together with, at least, some external affairs, so that I may the more readily give account of the office entrusted to me.

On the fourth Sunday in Advent, on the 21st of December, 1483, the feast of St. Thomas the Apostle, I was received as Master of the Ceremonies by the Reverend Father in Christ, Lord Adriano, Bishop of Ardicino della Porta. But I was admitted to the conduct of the ceremonies much later, that is on the 26th day of the month of January, 1484, by the authorities of the Apostolic Church, in place of the Reverend Father in Christ, Lord Agostino Patrizi Piccolomini, Canon of Siena, who was afterwards appointed to the churches of Pienza and Montalcino, and who retired from this post and office; and when his resignation was accepted, I was prepared for the post by these same authorities, through the most Holy Father and Lord in Christ, Sixtus IV, Pope by Divine Providence.

And for this I paid the aforesaid Lord Bishop of Pienza, together with the attendant expenses, a total of about 450 ducats, in gold of the Camera.

On Sunday, the 30th of May, 1484, the Lord Girolamo Riario, Count and Captain-general of the Holy Roman Church, and Gentilio Orsini, together with their men to the number of 3,000 or thereabouts, during the night surrounded the residence of the Very Reverend Father and Lord in Christ, Lord Giovanni of Santa Maria in Aquiro, commonly known as Cardinal-Deacon Colonna. The Cardinal's men who were within, bravely defended it for the space of about two hours. At length overcome by the count's men, who rushed in from the back and sides, they fled from the house. The count's men entered and plundered the house completely stripping it of all that was in it, even to the doors and windows. Finally they set fire to it and burned the residence and chambers of the cardinal, taking prisoner the Lord Lorenzo Colonna, prothonotary of the Apostolic See, together with several others, whom they brought to the Castle of San Angelo, where they kept them until they died.

On the same evening Pietro Valle and all his people fled from their houses and left them empty.

On Wednesday, the 1st of June, 1484, the Reverend Father and Lord the Prothonotary de Albergati of Bologna, governor of the city, together with Giovanni Francesco, the sheriff, and a great company of armed men and Lombards, appeared before the houses of the de Valle, where by order of the governor, the Lombards climbed to the roofs and stripped them off one after the other. With the exception of two they broke them all in. Some of the houses they practically razed to the ground, others were less injured, but none remained whole after these attacks.

On Wednesday, the 30th of June, 1484, the Reverend Father, Lord Lorenzo Colonna, prothonotary of the Apostolic See, who was in Holy Orders and in about the fortieth year of his age, was beheaded in the morning in the court within the first wall of the Castle of San Angelo. The Counts Girolamo and Gentile Virginio, so they say, stood and watched from the balcony of the castle. The corpse was then placed into an open wooden chest, in which it was to be buried, and the head was placed in position. The corpse was borne from the aforesaid castle to the Church of Santa Maria in Transpontina, where it could be reviewed by all who wished. Afterwards, during the night, it was brought to the Church of the Twelve Apostles, and given over to the Church for burial.

On Friday, the 2nd of July, 1484, in the morning, Giromalo, Count and Captain of the Church, together with his men, artillery, two large battering-engines and several small ones, went forth from the city to pitch his camp on the lands of the Colonna in order to besiege them, and he inflicted great injury upon them.

At the same time the Lord Domenico de Albergatis, prothonotary of Bologna, governor of the city, died from grief, it was said, at the downfall of the house of the Valle. The obsequies were performed in the Church of Santa Maria del Popolo.

On Thursday, the 12th of August, 1484, between the fourth and fifth hour of the night, or thereabouts, in the Vatican at St. Peter's, in an upper chamber, above the court in front of the library, there died our Most Holy Father and Lord in Christ, Lord Sixtus IV, Pope by Divine Providence. May the Almighty of His goodness deign to have mercy on his soul. Amen!

After his death, all the Most Reverend Lords, the Cardinals, who were present in the city, came to the palace, and passed through the chamber, wherein the deceased was lying on the bed, wearing a vestment over his cassock, a crucifix on his breast, his hands clasped together.

They paid profound respects to the deceased, such as are due from the cardinals; then they entered the great court near the said chamber, for the purpose of discussing what should be done.

The Bishop of Ceuta was appointed Captain, or Governor of the Capitol; the Bishop of Cervica, Captain of the Gate of the Palace of St. Peter; to each of the City Gates were appointed apostolic scriveners, together with solicitors and Roman citizens, and it was decided that all the princes, countries and officials should be informed of the Pope's decease.

Certain cardinals were appointed to guard the palace, and to transact any business which might present itself.  After the fifth hour, Giovanni Maria, my colleague, called upon me at my house, and I went with him to the aforesaid palace to make the necessary arrangements for the burial of the deceased.  But, prior to this, the Most Reverend Lord Vice-Chancellor had arrived at the palace, and according to custom he broke the seal used for the papal bulls, on which was engraved the name of the deceased pope.  Then, when the cardinals had assembled in the aforesaid place, they stopped up the mouth, nostrils, ears and anus of the deceased with silk, dipped in balm.  And, with the assistance of the regular penitentiaries of the Basilica of St. Peter, who meanwhile chanted the office for the dead in subdued, but distinct tones, standing round the corpse, they bore it away from this chamber to the lesser papal chamber, wrapped in the covering of the bed and in a certain cloth which formerly hung from the bed before the door of the aforesaid chamber, and there, about the tenth hour, they placed it naked in their midst, on a long table. The Abbot of San Sebastiano, the sacristan, had arranged a bier with torches, although that belonged rather to our office.

All the other rites were performed immediately, so to speak, as soon as the deceased had been borne away from the chamber; for, from that hour, until the 6th, despite all my diligence, I could not obtain one towel, linen cloth, or any vessel in which to place the wine and water and fragrant herbs for cleansing the deceased Pontiff, nor could I find drawers or a clean shirt in which to clothe him, although I several times besought the Cardinal of Parma, Pietro of Mantua, Lord Accorsio, Gregorio and Bartolommeo della Rovere, Giorgio his private sweeper, and Andrea his barber, who were all his private chamberlains, and of his household, and who had received the best of treatment at his hands. At length the cook furnished me with hot water and a cauldron in which he was wont to heat the water for washing the dishes, and the aforesaid Andrea, the barber, sent for the basin from his shop.

Thus the pope was washed, and since there was no linen cloth wherewith to dry him, I caused him to be dried with the shirt in which he had expired, torn in twain. I could not change the drawers in which he died, and in which he was washed, for there were no others. He was clothed in a doublet without a shirt, and a pair of shoes of pink cloth, furnished by the Bishop of Cervica, who was also his groom of the bed-chamber, and, unless my memory fails me, a damask vestment, either red or white. In this I erred, for he should have been buried in the habit of St. Francis, to whose Order he belonged, worn over the holy pontifical vestments. And, since he had no rochet, we placed on him the holy vestments over the aforementioned things; — the sandals, amice, alb, girdle, and the stole crossed over his breast (because I could not procure a pectoral cross), the tunic, dalmatic, gloves, the precious white chasuble, the pallium, the simple mitre, and the signet-ring with its valuable sapphire which the sacristan said was worth 300 ducats. Thus vested, we laid him on the bier which we arranged on the aforementioned table, with cushions at his head, and a pall of bro-cade, in the midst of the aforesaid chamber. There he remained until the hour of burial.

In the meanwhile, I entreated for wax candles, and with great difficulty about the fourteenth hour, these were produced to the number of twenty. When these had been brought, without any office having been said round the corpse, the crucifix and the acolytes going first, the penitentiaries and the chamberlains carried the deceased as far as the first large court, that is to say, of the palace. Here were the canons and the beneficiaries and the clergy of the Basilica of St. Peter; from that place the aforesaid canons bore the deceased to the high altar. The procession passed over the staircase and through the court, the way by which the cardinals are wont to descend when they go out through the principal gate of the palace to the central court-yard; thence, turning in the direction of the steps of the Basilica, we entered the church.

The deceased was placed before the altar on the first step, next his head was placed towards the altar, and his feet outside the iron rails, in order that those who wished might kiss them, and the gates of the rails were closed.

These were afterwards opened for a short time, and the deceased was placed nearer the altar, so that all could freely enter and depart, and some guardians were stationed there, lest his ring or any other possession should be stolen. He remained in that place until the first hour of the night, or thereabouts, when the shield-bearers bore him away, and we walked in front with the aforementioned twenty wax candles. Only eight cardinals followed. After them came the prelates, and the ambassadors, and a great many others.

After the deceased had been carried, as stated,

into the church, the cardinals withdrew; some went to the aforementioned palace, while others went to their homes.

When they had partaken of a refection, the cardinals entrusted to me the ordering of a coffin in which to bury the pope, and the arrangement for his burial in his new chapel of the choir of the canons and clergy of the aforesaid Basilica, which the deceased himself had ordered to be built in the same Basilica, about the middle of the same chapel, facing the principal altar, in the center, as they declared that the deceased had himself chosen this place for his burial.  I did this as I was ordered.

About the first hour of the night of Friday, 13th August, the body of the deceased was borne from the choir of the principal altar by the clergy of the said Basilica in a procession to the place of burial, and it was buried with all the vestments, precious ring and chasuble aforesaid.  There, as it lay in the tomb, in a long, wide coffin of nut-wood, which I had ordered, Lord Achilles, Bishop of Cervica, who was the only prelate there, together with a few clergy, chanted the *Miserere* and a prayer.  He sprinkled the deceased and the tomb with holy water, and we immediately covered the corpse with the pall.  Then, according to the command and express injunction of the College of the Most Reverend Lords the Cardinals, I forbade the canons and the clergy of the aforesaid

Basilica, under penalty of being deprived of their benefices, to allow any man to touch the deceased, or to remove the said signet-ring, or the chasuble, or anything else.

# II

## THE CONCLAVE WHICH CHOSE
## INNOCENT VIII

ON the last days (of August, 1484) the Very
Reverend Lords, the Cardinals, wishing to ap-
point four suitable persons as guardians of the
palace and of the conclave, as is the custom, commanded me through the Very Reverend Lord Vice-
Chancellor to write down the names of the prelates
of the Court and the ambassadors of the different
nations, and to present the list to them, those whom
they wished to have as guardians.   And this I did.

But we will briefly add how the arrangement of
the food and drink of the Very Reverend Lords, the
Cardinals, was managed, together with a description
of certain other things which were done in the conclave.

On behalf of the Very Reverend Lords, the Cardinals, before they entered the conclave, places situated near the palace, in which the conclave was to
be held, were chosen and arranged.   In these places
were the masters of the courts and the cooks of the
cardinals themselves, who prepared each meal.
Moreover, about the hours of luncheon and supper

the *magistri domorum*, the treasurers, came to the above-mentioned places from the houses of the cardinals, bringing wines, and with them came some of the chaplains, shield-bearers, and others, who were guarding the palaces of the cardinals. Then, when the hour had come, the shield-bearers walked in front, two by two, and the chaplains followed in their order, with stable-boys, one before and the other behind, who bore between them on their shoulders wooden vessels slung on a stick, containing the food and drink and bread of the cardinals.

When they arrived at the door of the second watch of the palace, the shield-bearers and the chaplains remained there together with the major-domo, and the stable boys with the wooden vessels went up the staircase as far as the third or fourth watch, and there, outside the door of the conclave, they set down the wooden vessels. This kind of wooden vessel has a lid with two keys, the one like unto the other; of these, the master of the court kept one, and the other was in the possession of those in the conclave who attended upon each Very Reverend Lord Cardinal.

The former, when he had placed the food and wine in the wooden vessel, having first made a list of each thing, closed the wooden vessel with the key, and, in the manner above described, despatched it to the conclave. There were two of these wooden vessels of which one was sent in the manner above described, and the other which was in the conclave was returned, and in this all the things taken out from the one that remained outside were placed, these things having been handed into the conclave through the hatch, and then each vessel was replaced in the chamber of the cardinal to whom it belonged.

I, or my colleague, summoned the members of the conclave of that cardinal to whom the wooden vessel belonged, and, when they approached with his empty wooden vessel, I opened the hatch of the door from within, and those of the fourth watch opened it from without, and the members of the conclave themselves from within, held out the wooden vessels to the custodians, who, when they had opened each wooden vessel, drew out everything from it and placed it upon the small table which stood in readiness there, near the door of the conclave; and there one of the custodians, appointed for this purpose by the others, inspected each, turning over the middle of the loaves and the soup, cutting open the fowls, tearing asunder the joints, the loaves and the tarts, whenever it seemed good to them, and looking through the glass bottles or decanters of wine. For the wine was sent or carried in uncovered glass bottles, not in flasks or any other vessel. But the soup was sent in as small jars as possible.

When they had carefully inspected each of the vessels the guardians themselves handed them to us clerks of the ceremonies through the hatch of the door. Moreover, we on receiving them placed them on our great sideboard, where the members of the conclave who were waiting received them, each placing them in his wooden vessel which he held in readiness there, wherein each of them carried the victuals to his chamber. When the food for supper arrived in the evening, the members of the conclave set forth vessels of silver and glass which they had taken in the morning upon our sideboard in the conclave and I returned them empty to the stable-boys who were waiting from without. But we clerks of the ceremonies placed the bread and the wine and the salt meats, and other things that would keep in our vessels which we had brought to the conclave for this purpose. Moreover, I had brought a small bottle in which to collect the wine, and a big basket for the bread and the like, and this I placed in the chamber of the doctors, which led to the privies in the corner near the door of the conclave. But the other things, that is to say, the soups, joints or fresh fish and the like, which were left over, we gave to the aforesaid custodians, and I did the same in the morning with regard to the vessels received in the evening.

The stable-boys or the other servants of the cardinals waited near the second watch in the morning and in the evening, and they were informed by us and by the custodians at what hour the food should be brought, and when they had been informed they brought it, and not before; for a fixed time could not be assigned to them because the cardinals dispatched their business sometimes sooner, sometimes later. The aforesaid custodians did not deal with the said food in any given order, but he who came first with the food was the first to be released, whether he were first or last in importance or whether he were the *familiar* of any cardinal whatsoever. The same custodians appointed between themselves every day, two of the fourth watch, one for lunch and the other for supper, to examine the food in the fashion described above, whilst the others assisted him. No member of the conclave at any time, or for any cause whatsoever, was admitted to the hatch, whether this were open or closed, even for the purpose of speaking to any one from without, except with the express leave of the college. If any letters came to the college, which could not be received through the opening of the hatch, we opened the hatch, and having taken the letters we quickly closed it again. But we gave the letters, I, or my colleague, to the College of Cardinals, if they were all assembled together, or we told two or three of the senior cardinals that we had letters for the college, and that, if it pleased them, we could give them to the Dean of Cardinals.

But, if any one from outside desired to send information within, he spoke with the hatch closed, and one of us two, having heard what he had to say, referred it to the Dean of the Cardinals, and to three or four of the other cardinals, he being also notified of this.  When the hatch was opened to take in the food and to send forth the vessels, he took great care to prevent any member of the conclave, not only from approaching the hatch, but also from making any sign, which would be received from any one from without.  When the sacristan celebrated a public mass, all the members of the conclave, or those who wished, might hear the said mass, but they must stand outside the doors of the smaller chapel in which mass was celebrated, which doors led into the first and second court of the conclave, and, whilst mass was being celebrated, no man knocked at the door of the conclave.  Likewise, whilst the votes were being examined, when mass was over, and when the stools had been arranged for each of the cardinals with a folio of papyrus, paper, and reed-pen, ink and two or three small candles, all returned to the larger chapel, in which they were all confined by us, the clerks of the ceremonies, the cardinals being in congregation.  I guarded the door of the first court, so that, between the third court, in which the congregations were held, and myself, there was the second middle court, and, when they wished to summon me, one or other of the cardinals rang the bell; some took their meals alone in their cells, others with two, three, or four others, or several together.

When luncheon was over, on the aforesaid Saturday, August 28th, various intrigues were set on foot, and at length the votes of about seventeen of the

Very Reverend Lords, the Cardinals, were given in favor of the Very Reverend Lord Cardinal of Molfetta, who, the following evening, before the sixth hour of the night, began, at the request of certain of the cardinals, to sign petitions in his chamber; having knelt down on one knee, he signed the petitions placed before him on a certain small box; some of the cardinals who were asking and waiting for these signatures stood round; while this was happening, the Very Reverend Lord Cardinal of Siena came up, and seeing this, he said, with a smile: "This is an inversion of the right order of things; the Pope is signing petitions on his knees, and we, the petitioners, stand upright."

On Tuesday, the 29th of August, the day of the Decollation of Saint John the Baptist, very early in the morning, the Very Reverend Lord Cardinal of San Marco, from motives of piety, celebrated a public mass in the small chapel, as indeed he did on the two following days; thereupon, about the tenth hour, when all the cardinals were standing in order in the aforementioned small chapel in their capes and with their croziers as on the day before, our sacristan celebrated the mass of the Holy Ghost with commemoration of the faithful departed, as on the day before, and, when this was over, we prepared a small table and stools with their appurtenances, as on the day before, and we all went out of the same chapel, leaving the cardinals there alone, and all the

members of the conclave were confined in the larger
chapel. And, meanwhile, the latter put their possessions together, asked for their chambers, and each
one collected all his things, with the exception of the
members of the conclave of the Cardinal of Molfetta,
who left the chamber of their lord with the possessions of the members of the conclave. The cardinals
in the small chapel made examination of the votes as
on the day before, but there was no mention made of
the accession.

When the examination of the votes was over, it
was found that the Very Reverend Lord Giovanni,
of the title of Santa Cecilia, Cardinal-priest of Molfetta, had sufficient votes. Therefore, unanimously,
by all the cardinals, and by the whole college
of the said cardinals without any protest, he
was admitted and received as Supreme Pontiff of the Holy Roman and Catholic Church, and
as a sign of his admittance, the cardinals laid down
their croziers before him, and invested him with the
cape over the rochet. And they placed him in the
magnificent seat of the chamber between the altar
and the aforesaid small table, and they placed upon
his finger the signet-ring of Pope Sixtus IV, of
blessed memory, which ring the sacristan had in
readiness for this purpose; and when he had been
received as Pope, thus seated, he himself chose for
himself the name of Innocent VIII, Pope.

# III

## THE FIRST YEARS OF THE REIGN OF INNOCENT VIII

ON Sunday, the Fifth of Lent, the 20th of March, 1485, the Pontiff, who was lying sick in bed in the room in which he generally slept, and clothed over his shirt in a robe reaching to the arms only, was visited by all the cardinals, by the Count of Dauphiné, the Ambassador to the French King, and by Giovanni Maria, my colleague, and by me, and the private chamberlains, but by no other. When we were stationed in his presence, the Pope, holding the Rose [1] in his right hand, gave it to the Count of Dauphiné aforesaid, who was kneeling by the bed, with these words from the book: " Accipe rosam," etc., as at the ceremonial. This done, the Count kissed the Pope's hand, but not his foot, because the Pope's feet were covered. The count then withdrew, and with him all the cardinals who further attended him as far as his lodging, that is, to the palace of the Orsini, in the Campo dei Fiori, he riding behind, as usual, between the two chief cardinal-deacons.

[1] The Golden Rose (Rosa Aurea), a rose made of gold and consecrated by the Pope, which is presented to such princes as have rendered special services to the church.

19

On Thursday, the 17th of November, 1485, the Reverend Father in Christ, Achille Marescotto of Bononia, Bishop of Cervia, who on the preceding Saturday, the 12th of this month, had returned in health and spirits to the city, and on the preceding Tuesday, the 15th, had fallen ill of the plague, on the night of this day breathed his last. On the same night he was in the Basilica of St. Peter handed over for ecclesiastical burial with no ceremonies. May his soul rest in peace.

On Friday, the 22nd of September, 1486, before the hour of the consistory, on the space above the steps, before the Basilica of St. Peter, upon a platform erected for the purpose, were assembled the following persons: the Reverend Father Tito, Lord Bishop of Castres in the Patrimony, vested in amice, alb, girdle, stole, red cope and plain mitre, seated on a folding-stool; the Reverend Father Pietro di Vicentia, Lord Auditor of the Apostolic Chamber of the Court of Causes; N. di Parma, fiscal procurator; and several others, with Friar Gabriel di Fontaria of Piacenza, a professed religious of the Order of the Canons Regular of St. Augustine, one who has received all the orders, up to and including that of priest. Wearing his vestments, and standing facing the people, the Lord Giacomo, the notary, read the summary of the process against the said Gabriel, and the sentence pronounced against him, and the commission for his degradation. When these had been

read, the said Lord Bishop degraded him, in accordance with the order given in the Pontifical, upon the
strength of the commission given.

After he had been degraded, the apparitor led
him away to the Castle of Soldano, and on Saturday,
23rd September, about one o'clock, the said degraded
person was hanged in the Campo dei Fiori, suffering
the death penalty with great patience and devotion,
as the witnesses reported.  At the head of the cord
by which he was hanged was fastened gold foil, as a
sign that he was a noted robber.

The same morning, in the Campidolio, was hanged
for theft a certain Jew, who had become a Christian.
He refused to have the cross before him, or a Christian to comfort him in the faith of Christ, but wished
to die in Judaism, and thus he was hanged and died.
His accomplice, another Jew, also in prison, ought
to have been hanged with him, but he threw himself
into the sewer, from which he was taken out alive
on the same day, and then was also hanged.

On the Second Sunday in Advent, 10th December,
1486, in the larger chapel the Reverend Father in
Christ, Lorenzo, Lord Archbishop of Benevento,
celebrated the solemn mass in cardinal's vestments,
as was done at the first Sunday.  The Pope and the
cardinals were present.  Four prayers were recited:
the first, of the day; the second, *Deus, qui salutis*,
etc.: the third, against the heathen; the fourth, for
the Pope.

The Procurator of the Order of Friars Minor preached the sermon, concerning which there was a great dispute between him and the Master of the Palace. For the Master of the Palace had told me not to allow him to preach, because he had not shown him the sermon first. He excused himself, saying that he had only returned to the city in the evening of the day before yesterday, and this morning, when he sought him at his house, he could not find him. The Cardinal of S. Pietro in Vincoli, protector of the Order of Minors, said to the Master of the Palace that the procurator was an approved man, allow the procurator to preach. The master aforesaid had previously, however, come over to this view, and therefore he ought not to trouble. At length I asked our Most Holy Lord, who said that I should in the opinion of the Most Reverend Lord Cardinal aforesaid, although he did not give his consent. All the other observances were as usual.

I think that the procurator did not show his sermon to the master because of what he intended to say; for he said in it that the Blessed Virgin Mary was conceived without original sin, which is in accordance with the doctrine of the Scotists, but contrary to that of the Thomists, to which latter party the Master of the Palace belongs.

On the Fourth Sunday in Advent, the Vigil of the Nativity of Our Savior, 24th December, 1486, the Pope came to the chapel with only four cardinals, the Cardinal of Naples and three deacons.  The Cardinal of Naples held the boat for the incense, as there was no priest.  Then the priests came and there were all the usual observances.  The cardinals made the reverence, and wrongly, for they were to make it the same evening, and it ought not to be made twice in a day; it was done, however, inadvertently. There was no sermon.  The mass ended, because I was hindered with the *pax*, and my colleagues did not notice.  No indulgence was asked for, nor was one granted by the Pope.  No one noticed, however, and therefore there was no blame nor scandal whatever.

On Thursday, 24th May, 1487, the Feast of the Ascension of Our Lord Jesus Christ, the Most Reverend Lord Cardinal of St. Clement performed the office in the Basilica of the chief of the Apostles in white vestments, the Pope being present.  The Duke of Ferrara bore the borders of the Pope's cope to the steps of the palace, where the Pope ascended his chair, and was carried in state to the Basilica aforesaid in the usual way.

Before the entrance of the aforesaid Basilica were kneeling naked two citizens of Bononia.  One of these, several months before, when Officer of Justice of the State of Bononia, had caused two priests, one secular, the other a regular, member of the Order of St. Francis, who were condemned to die by his sentence, to be taken and hanged for their crimes.

Because they were not under his jurisdiction our
Most Holy Lord had deprived him of this and all
his offices, and had caused his officials to be punished
with fitting penalties.  Of these, four have recently
done penance, and one was here with his superior
this morning.  Around these two men there stood,
vested in priestly vestments, all the penitentiaries
of the aforesaid Basilica, holding rods or staves in
their hands, and smiting them whilst reciting the
psalm, *Miserere mei Deus*, to the end.  When it was
ended one of these penitentiaries admonished them
in the usual words.  Then our Most Holy Lord laid
upon the aforesaid penitents, as a penance, that of
their own personal estate they should found in Bononia one chapel, and endow it for one benefice, and
sufficiently for one priest who should celebrate on
each Sunday and Feast a mass in the chapel; this
mass the first citizen should hear and be present at
from beginning to end, kneeling and holding a lighted
candle in his hand, and should pray and entreat God
for the souls of the two priests whom, as told above,
he had had hanged.  This penance he accepted.

On Thursday, the 28th of June, 1487, the Vigil
of the Apostles Peter and Paul, there were solemn
pontifical vespers in the Basilica of the chief of the
Apostles.  The cardinals and all the clergy came
from the robing-room to the said Basilica in their
vestments, and wrongly, for they ought to have come
in their capes, and after the cardinals had made the

reverence in their capes they and the clergy ought then to have taken their vestments.

But the cardinals desired to come in this way. I could not prevent this, but I would not allow them to bear the baldacchino over the Pontiff until they carried the censer and the candlesticks into the Basilica. The cardinals only made the reverence, and not the clergy, in the usual way. After the reverence, the Pope began the vespers. The other observances were conducted as usual, except that some of the cardinals wished to come in their vestments and to escort our lord, so that from the one unfitting circumstance several others resulted. They came outside the Basilica, and there they laid aside their vestments and took their capes, and wrongly. Though I saw it I could not resist their pleasure and passed the matter over in silence.

On Friday, the 29th of June, 1487, the Feast of the Apostles Peter and Paul, our Most Holy Lord came to the church in procession under the baldacchino in the morning, escorted by the cardinals and clergy in their vestments and by the officials in white. This and everything else was carried out this morning in the usual way. Water was brought to the Pontiff for washing his hands: firstly, by one of the ambassadors of the King of England; secondly, by a senator; thirdly, by the Count of Tendilla, the ambassador of the King of Spain; fourthly, by the Emperor of Constantinople.

On Monday, the 4th of February, 1488, there was a public consistory in the first and larger hall of the Apostolic Palace at which the four ambassadors of the Most Serene King Maximilian did homage and reverence to our Most Holy Lord in the name of the king and his son Philip, for the dukedoms of Austria and Burgundy, and other of his principalities and dominions.

This done, the two deacon-cardinals came to assist our Most Holy Lord while all the other cardinals and clergy remained in their places. There then entered the consistory and passed on to the second hall about a hundred Moors, each with large iron rings on their necks, and all bound together with a long chain and ropes, and dressed all in the same costume. These were followed by an ambassador of the King and Queen of Spain, who knelt before our Most Holy Lord, kissing his foot only, and presented the letters of the aforesaid king and queen, written in the Spanish tongue. The Reverend Father Antoniotto, Lord Bishop of Auray, the datary, read these letters aloud, to the effect that the King and Queen of Spain were sending to His Holiness a hundred Moors, a part of the spoils taken in their victory of the preceding summer over the King of Granada, which Moors they presented as a gift to His Holiness, and offered, moreover, to send others should it so please His Holiness.

On Tuesday, the 10th of March, 1489, the Reverend Jean, Lord Bishop of Aubusson, Cardinal of Angers, with others brought it about that Zizim,[1] brother of the great Turk, came to Rome. This Zizim, fleeing from the wrath and persecution of his brother, came to the Island of Rhodes in the year 1480, or thereabouts, under the safe conduct of the Grand-Master of the Knights of Jerusalem.

Hence, for his own greater safety, because his brother had sought in many ways and was daily seeking to take his life, Zizim had been sent into France by the Reverend Lord Pierre of Ghent, grand-master of the knights aforesaid, first to Bouillon, then to Bourgneuf, the castle which he had inherited from his father. Thence, under the escort of his nephew, Guido de Blanchefort, Prior of Alvernia, the prince came to Rome.

On Friday, the 13th of March, 1489, about eight o'clock, Zizim, brother of the Sultan of Turkey, entered the city on one of the white horses called *chinei.* By command of the Pope he was met by the households of the cardinals without the clergy, that is to say, the chaplains and esquires only. In the same way the Pope's household came with only the chamberlains and esquires. Within the gate they all received him in their midst, removing and immediately replacing their caps. But the Turkish prince,

---

[1] See Appendix.

who had his head covered after the fashion of his
people with a large white turban, uncovered to nobody, but merely bowed slightly.

The first of the household of each cardinal received him in some such words as these:— " The Most
Reverend My Lord the Cardinal by command of our
Most Holy Lord the Pope, has sent this his household, to meet Your Highness, rejoicing at your
safe arrival," except the Lord Pietro, Spanish cauda-
tory to the Most Reverend, the Lord Cardinal of
San Marco, who welcomed him in some such form of
words as this:— " Most Serene Prince, the Most
Reverend My Lord the Cardinal of San Marco, was
filled with joy when he learned that your Highness
was to come to the city: wherefore, to show the pleasure which he feels, he has sent his household to honor
your entry.  His Reverend Lordship prays God, the
all-good, all-great and all-powerful, that Your
Majesty's coming here may be happy and prosperous, and may have such result as all good men desire,
and to this end he congratulates Your Highness upon
your safe arrival, and at the same time places himself
and all that he has, at your free disposal."

After this reception, the Turkish prince aforementioned, rode between Francesco Cibó, son of our
Most Holy Lord the Pope, who was on his right
hand, and the Prior of Alvernia, nephew of the new
cardinal, on his left; and although a senator and
several lay ambassadors, namely the ambassadors of

King Ferdinand, Venice and others, also kinsmen
of the Pontiff, received the said Turkish prince, yet
because the Prior of Alvernia, who claimed to be the
ambassador of the King of France and to have charge
of the said prince, would not give place to the senator
and ambassadors, they all withdrew except the senator, who rode before us.    In this order we came to
the Apostolic Palace, where the prince was entertained in the Apostolic apartments in which the
emperor and kings and other great princes are received.    The route was over the Bridge of Bartolommeo, or the Island by the Ghetto, across the
Campo dei Fiori straight to the aforesaid palace.    A
great crowd of people stood around and watched his
entry.

First rode the households of the cardinals, then
the households of the knights, and the knights who
had escorted the Turkish prince from France: the
household of the prince, about ten in number, exclud-
ing his other retainers, the chief of whom had at his
right hand, the ambassador of the Sultan, of whom
we shall speak below: the esquires of the Pope, the
senator with certain nobles, the men-at-arms, the
herald of the French king and of the masters of
ceremonies.    On my left was the interpreter of the
Turkish prince, and the prince himself, who rode
between Francesco Cibó and the prior aforesaid, the
*Turchopellerius* of Rhodes, four of the nobles
in the household of the prince, the Pope's cham-

berlains, and all the Rhodians after the chamberlain.

The prince dismounted in the court of the palace, where the cardinals pass, and from there he went up through the great hall, and was conducted to the aforementioned apartments where he was entertained and guarded by the troops aforesaid.

During the past months there came to the city an ambassador from the Grand Turk sent to the Pope on account of the Turkish prince received to-day. When he learned that the prince would make his entry into the city to-day, he went on horseback to meet him outside the Porta Portese, with his household on foot, of whom there were about ten. For the Turkish prince was waiting on horseback near the city walls and the river outside the said gate for the hour appointed for his entry. The prior and *Turchopellerius* aforesaid went to meet this ambassador, who was waiting outside the said gate to prevent his approaching the prince; but when Francesco Cibó learned that the ambassador wished to approach the prince, he gave orders that he should be allowed.

Thereupon the prior and *Turchopellerius* aforesaid commanded the retainers of the ambassador, who were holding their bows taut, though not with arrows to them, to lay aside their bows and so to approach unarmed, which they did. Then they came up, the ambassador on horseback and his men on foot, and

when he was within sight of the prince and about
forty paces away, the ambassador got down from
his horse, and with a very noble carriage, approached
to within fifteen paces.   Then coming forward about
five paces, he bowed himself to the ground, touching
it with his head upon the right side; then rising
and coming forward three or four paces more, he
knelt upon his right knee, touched the ground with
his right hand, and then kissed his own hand.   Then
rising again and coming as many paces forward to
the prince, he knelt before him and embraced his
horse by the right or left foot, and the prince by his
right foot, and at the same time he kissed the prince's
foot.   Then rising he kissed his right knee thrice,
and when the prince stretched out his right hand to
his neck he kissed his garments in the same way.
All this the ambassador appeared to do so sincerely
that he seemed to all to be weeping.   But the prince
made him no sign, but waited for him as a prince
unmoved, and neither spoke a word to the other, but
when the ambassador had made his salutations in
a single word as he stood there before him, the
prince bade him mount his horse; his own horse
was first brought for him to mount, and then he
retired a whole pace from the prince to mount, and
returned on horseback before the prince.   Meanwhile there came one of the prince's household, who
embraced in turn each member of the ambassador's
household, while they knelt one by one before the

prince, touched the ground with the right hand, and kissed their right hand; then kneeling they embraced the horse's foot, and the prince's right foot; then kissed first his foot and afterward his knee. In the fewest possible words, the Turkish prince and the ambassador made peace, and thus afterward the prince made his entry into the city in the order described above.

On Saturday, the 14th of March, 1489, notice was given of a public consistory to be held in the first great hall of the Apostolic Palace at one o'clock.

Escorted by Francesco Cibo and the Prior of Alvernia, preceded by men-at-arms and followed by his fourteen servitors and soldiers, the Turkish prince came to the consistory into the presence of the Pontiff. Now though it was said that the prince would do reverence to the Pontiff in the Turkish fashion by touching the ground with his hand and then kissing his hand, he refused to do so. Indeed he merely bowed his covered head very slightly to the Pontiff, so slightly that the bow could scarcely be seen or recognized as such. He went up to the Pontiff and, standing erect, embraced him and kissed him lightly upon the right arm, all the time keeping his head covered. Then, standing before the Pontiff, he said, by means of an interpreter, that he was glad to have come into the presence of the Pontiff, and asked him to be mindful of the fact and to afford him protection; adding that when a time and place were appointed, he would tell him of other matters in private. The Pontiff replied that he had already taken the measures for his safety and welfare wherewith his Highness had been brought to Rome, and that his Highness ought in no wise to mistrust, but to dwell in peace, seeing that all things were ordered for a wise end. For these words the prince thanked His Holiness, stating that he felt full confidence in them.

Then the prince withdrew from before the Pontiff and embraced all the cardinals as they stood in their places and kissed them on or near the right shoulder. Meanwhile the other members of his household came into the presence of the Pontiff, and one after the other in turn, knelt upon the throne, and touching the ground with the right hand kissed it; they then embraced the feet of the Pope, as well as his cope and vestments, and on bended knee kissed these and followed the prince, their patron. He, having embraced all the cardinals except the two who remained with the Pontiff to assist him, without bearing himself in any other fashion, or making any other sort of salutation to the Pontiff, returned to his apartments, escorted as before. Then the Pontiff rose and returned to his apartment in the usual way.

# IV

## THE LAST YEARS OF THE REIGN OF INNOCENT VIII

ON Wednesday, the 25th of March, 1489, the Feast of the Annunciation of the Blessed Virgin Mary; in the morning I had a long conversation with the Pontiff. I told him it was not right to wear a white cape, but he ought properly to wear a red cape with a violet stole, not a red one, also that the cardinals should follow, and not precede His Holiness. But His Holiness said that Sixtus IV, his predecessor, used to ride at this season with a white cape, and the Lord Vice-Chancellor, listening to no argument, said the cardinals should precede. And this was done, although not fittingly.

On Saturday, the 27th of June, 1489, the Noble Lord Nicola Orsino, Count of Pitigliano, Siena, and Nola, who was to be Captain-General of the Holy Roman Church, and to make his entry into the city with his household and intimate friends, but not with the households of the cardinals, entered the Apostolic Palace by the viridario to see our Most Holy Lord, by whom he was graciously received. Then the said count who by studying the stars had conceived the

35

idea that he might assume the insignia of his captaincy under favorable auspices to-day, sought and obtained from our Most Holy Lord permission for the said insignia to be given to him.

On the Sunday night, 15th September, 1489, Signor Domenico Gentile of Viterbo, apostolic writer, Francesco Maldente, canon of Forli and Conrado, also Battista of Spell, notary of the Apostolic Camera, Lorenzo Signoretto, writer in the *Register of Bulls*, and Bartolommeo Budello, procurator of the Penitentiary, were successively taken and detained in the Castle of San Angelo on a charge of forging apostolic letters. The Lord Domenico aforesaid confessed that he had forged about fifty apostolic letters or bulls, containing various matters, in the following way:— The Lord Francesco would discover matters to be despatched and agree with the parties upon the sum which they were to pay after the despatch of letters. When the agreement had been made and a bank named by the party for paying the sum agreed upon to be paid when the letters were presented to the bank, then he would despatch one that was expected, or some matter that would pass easily through all the offices by the royal way. When this was done, the Lord Domenico aforementioned washed out all the writing of the bull, or that part which he did not want, with a certain fluid, restored the paper with flour and stiffened it again. Afterward he wrote on it the matter concerning which Francesco had agreed with the party, leaving in the bull the names of the rescribendary, computators, and other officials. More often he changed the stamp, and put on another, according to the nature of the matter. He also used different inks. That with which he wrote the first matter to be despatched in the proper way was made of gum or some other material, but was certainly indelible. But the other, which he used to write over the bull that had been erased, was ordinary ink. In this way they gave forged bulls to the parties.

Within about two years they had despatched divers matters, for example, dispensations to one or two benefices for Friars of the Orders of Mendicants, unions of many benefices to the incomes of certain abbots with permission to rule these in an order changeable at pleasure, a dispensation for a certain priest of the Diocese of Rouen, who had married a wife, to the effect that he might lawfully keep her and many others for which they had received sometimes a hundred, two hundred, two hundred and fifty, and two thousand ducats, as is related in the process instituted against them.

The said Francesco also made confession, and on Sunday, the 18th of October, at about nine in the evening, they both were led from the castle aforementioned to the Castle of Soldano, and before they reached that place they believed they were condemned to death. For the auditor of the Camera, the

Bishop of Cesena, and the Lord Bartolommeo Deol-
pito, first apostolic notary and governor of the city,
who in their official capacity had prosecuted them,
told the said Francesco that if he named his fellow-
accomplices our Most Holy Lord would be pleased
to bestow the office of abbreviator upon him and set
him at liberty, and he believing that he would do this
accused the abovenamed and several others. On behalf of the Lord Domenico, his father who had attended our Most Holy Lord in the first illness of his
pontificate, and his two brothers interceded most
earnestly with the cardinals and other influential men
in the city for his life. But no one could prevail
upon our Most Holy Lord. So, after they had
been established in the said castle, they were told
that they were to die on the morrow; and therefore
were bidden to take heed to the salvation of their
souls, and priests were sent to them to hear their
confession and strengthen them in the faith.

On Monday, the 19th of October, 1489, there was
a consistory and the auditor of the Camera aforesaid
with the governor came to the Castle of Soldano
where they passed definite sentence against the said
Domenico and Francesco, degraded them, deprived
them of office and emoluments, and handed them over
to the secular court. Then mass was celebrated in
the said castle, at which the said Domenico and Francesco were present, and at the close they received
the holy communion from the hands of the celebrant;

LAST YEARS OF INNOCENT VIII 39

after this they were led to the Piazza di San Pietro, where a platform had been erected in a space not far from the lowest step, four rods long, three wide, and one high, or thereabouts. There the said Francesco who was a priest was robed in full vestments in the usual way. Then the summary of the case was read by the notary, Antonio of Paimpol. After the reading of it, Francesco was degraded and given over to the secular court into the hands of Ambrosino, the apparitor.

After he had been given over, Domenico who had only the first tonsure was robed in a surplice and degraded from that rank by the Father Pietro Paolo, Lord Bishop of Santa Agata, who vested himself in stole and cope upon the platform, and put on in front a plain alb over the rochet. After his degradation Domenico was given over to the court and the said apparitor. Their heads were not shaved otherwise than they had been before, nor were they stripped of the clothes in which they came from the castle, because of their office and because such was the pleasure of the Bishop of Cesena, the auditor.

After this the aforesaid having been degraded were placed upon a chariot which stood ready there, Domenico on the right and Francesco on the left. In front of them were seated a friar of the Order of Minors, their confessor, in accordance with the observance in parts of France, and another of the society of the Misericordia who held a crucifix and was robed in the garb of that society with his face covered. Behind the degraded ones were erected two rods, and to the top of them cords were fastened, on which were hung four of the bulls despatched and forged by them. In this way they were conducted by the Bridge of San Angelo past the Castle of Soldano and hard by the house of the Cardinal of Ascanio, past the Hospital of the Germans, close to the house of the Lord Falco by the Pario straight to another street, thence by the bridge to the Campo dei Fiori, where near the corner by the steps and the Taberna Vacca, so-called, the place of execution had been prepared in the form of a hut, having a wooden pillar erected in the center, and surrounded by piled-up faggots. To the upper part of the column had been fixed two ropes. Below the ropes two stools were placed upon the ground for the accused and another on the other side of the column for the lictor, and around the shed outside many piles of logs.

When the aforementioned degraded persons reached the said place of execution, they got down from the cart, and entered the hut, where in the guise and clothes in which they were brought there, they ascended the two stools prepared for them. The lictor put ropes upon their neck of which they were scarcely conscious, for the confessor and the other friar who bore the crucifix were continually strengthening them in Christ. When the ropes had been placed in position, the lictor's assistants drew away the stools from beneath their feet and thus they were hanged and gave up the ghost. After they were dead they were taken down from the pillar, stripped to their shirts and placed in a sitting position upon the said stools, propped against the pillar, and bound to the column with the chain beneath their arms. Then the fire was kindled and their bodies burned. The lictor heaped up the logs many times until after the hour of vespers, that the bodies might be entirely consumed, and thus the fire lasted until the following morning.

On the following day, about the hour of vespers, ashes, in which many of the bones were still found, were collected by certain of the society of Misericordia with a broom, placed in a sack in a new chest, and with the cross and the usual procession was borne by the said society to the church appointed for the purpose and buried.

On Wednesday, the 19th of May, 1490, the Vigil of the Ascension of Our Lord Jesus Christ, there were pontifical vespers in the larger chapel of the Apostolic Palace, the Pope being present and performing the office. When the cardinals had made the usual salutation to him there arose a contention between the ambassadors of the Kings of Naples and of Scotland, and of Venice, Milan and the Kingdom of Florence on the other hand, who said they ought not to be divided or separated from the ambassador of the Duke of Milan and the ambassadors of Otho, Albert, and George, Dukes of Bavaria, who stationed themselves above the Venetian ambassadors, whereat the Venetian and Florentine ambassadors straightway withdrew in wrath. The ambassadors of Ferdinand, King of Naples, and of the King of Scotland still persisted in the dispute and by special command of the Pope I ordered them both to leave the chapel, which they did immediately.

The vespers ended, His Holiness spoke with the cardinals, whom he called round him in a circle in the said chapel, upon the precedence of the personages aforesaid. Then he instructed me to notify the ambassadors of the Kings of Scotland and Bavaria not to come to the chapel on the morrow, and to inform them that on the next Friday His Holiness would bring this question of precedence before the consistory.

On Friday, the 28th of May, 1490, our Most Holy Lord, learning that the ambassador of the King of Naples was preparing to come to the vespers on the Vigil of Pentecost and take his place by armed force, instructed me to report this to the Lord Cardinals of Angers, Lisbon, San Angelo, Siena, and the Vice-Chancellor that they might consider what should be done in the matter and what course to pursue with regard to the ambassadors in this question of pre-

cedence, and that they should come to deliberate
with His Holiness on the morrow in his chamber before the vespers. This I did.

Therefore on Saturday, the 29th of May, 1490,
the Vigil of Pentecost, a private meeting of the cardinals was held in the presence of the Pontiff in
his chamber from before eight till nine in
the evening, and finally by the Pope's instructions
given in the said meeting, the ambassadors of the
King of Scotland and of the Dukes of Bavaria were
asked by the Bishop of Tournai to withdraw on that
evening, and to leave the other ambassadors undis-
turbed and that on the morrow the Pope would give
them a place. The ambassadors of Scotland and
Bavaria, however, refused altogether to accept this
arrangement unless the other ambassadors withdrew
with them, which was done; and they all withdrew,
both citramontanes and ultramontanes, and were all
bidden to absent themselves from the chapel on the
morrow, and this they all observed.

On Tuesday, the 10th of April, 1492, before morning, a knight from Florence came to the Cardinal
de' Medici with letters from Pietro announcing sad
tidings. They reported that on Sunday, about four
in the morning, Lorenzo de' Medici, citizen of Florence, father of the said cardinal, had breathed his
last at Careggi, an estate belonging to the said
Lorenzo, distant about twelve miles from Florence.
The cardinal had been informed of his father's death

by the Lord Falco, treasurer-general of our Most
Holy Lord the Pope, who, upon learning of the death
of the said Lorenzo, visited the cardinal in the morning. He had all ornaments and all coverings removed from his walls and couches and ordered black
caps to be given to all the members of his household.
The cardinal himself put on a tunic of dark violet
and had all seats of brocade and velvet removed
from his apartments, retaining only those covered
with red leather and the usual stools. He had a
valise made of dark violet cloth without arms upon
it, and he kept upon his tables as well as upon the
buffet and the couches, only coverings of rascia.
All his servants he had dressed in black.

Friday, the 4th of May, 1492, there their Most
Reverend Lordships the Vice-Chancellor, and the
Cardinals assembled in the papal chamber of the
Apostolic Palace at St. Peter's.

The Sultan of Constantinople sent by his ambassador who had just reached Ancona on his mission,
the head of the spear with which it was said that
the side of our Lord Jesus Christ was pierced as He
hung upon the cross. At the close of the congregation aforesaid the cardinals proceeded to consider
with what ceremonies and observances this spear-
head should be received, and they agreed that the
question should be referred to our Most Holy Lord.

In the congregation various points were brought
up and touched upon in relation to this matter. For,

while some were of the opinion that the gift should be received with all solemnity and reverence, and in the same manner as the head of St. Andrew the Apostle in the time of Pope Pius II of happy memory, others asserted on the contrary that they had seen the point of the said spear in Nuremberg, where it was exposed each year on the day which is the Feast of the Spear, and others in other States, as in Paris, for example, where it was kept in the king's chapel. The latter, therefore, thought that it should be received from the hands of the ambassador bringing it by our Most Holy Lord in his own apartment, in presence of all or some of the Most Reverend Lord Cardinals, without any solemnity, and that we should be sent to Nuremberg, Paris and elsewhere to ascertain the truth, and examine the documents at Paris, and also at Nuremberg, if they happen to have any apostolic letters there, from which the truth of the matter may be learned. From some chronicles it appears that the spear-point was given in pledge by Baldwin II, then Emperor of Constantinople, to the Venetians, and with their consent to Louis IX, King of France; in others, that, from some very old chronicles, it appeared that the spear-head was kept at Constantinople, and preserved there until this day, public honored and venerated by all, and that there are several witnesses, still living, who had seen it there before the siege of Constantinople and since. They averred that the Venetians sent with all diligence to the house of a certain citizen in Constantinople, who had received the spear-head during the siege of the town, and offered him fifteen thousand ducats for it. Then again they sent to the Grand Turk who had received it from the said citizen, and offered him seventy thousand ducats for it, but still were not able to get it. Others again said that in the receiving of this relic, three points should be considered, namely, the gift, the recipient, and the giver, who is the arch enemy of our faith, and that it would be more natural to suppose that this was done in a spirit of mockery and derision, than from any other motive.

All these and many other remarks upon the subject were duly considered and the majority of the cardinal-priests inclined to the opinion that the spear-head aforesaid should be received by our Most Holy Lord from the Turkish ambassador without any solemnity, and that the truth should then be inquired into, at Nuremberg or at Paris, as to whether it were the true spear-head or some other. Then, if this fact should be satisfactorily settled, it could be announced, and the relic conveyed in procession with all veneration and solemnity to some church, at the pleasure of our Most Holy Lord; while, on the other hand, if perhaps this relic should be received in a solemn manner, and it were afterwards discovered that the true spear-head was elsewhere, the Apostolic See might be involved in contumely or confusion.

However, our Most Holy Lord determined and ordained that the relic be solemnly received. And for this purpose he deputed Lord Nicola Cibo, Archbishop of Arles, the Bishop of Foligno and his domestic clergy to go to Ancona, and there receive the relic from the hands of the Turkish ambassador, and bring it thence to Rome with a procession drawn from the several states and territories lying along the route. That this might be the more conveniently done, they were given a casket of crystal from the Pope's sacristy and a horse, together with a covered chest and other trappings in which the Host is borne when the Pope rides out in full pontificals, with a lantern to carry a light perpetually before it.

On the 29th of May, 1492, about the hour of Vespers, the Count of Pitigliano, captain of the Church, Francesco Cibo, the Pope's son, and the Roman nobles left the city by the Porta Viridarii and hastened by way of the meadows towards the Ponte Milvio to meet the Turkish ambassador, but he in the meantime had crossed the bridge aforesaid and was riding towards the Porta del Popolo.

When I saw the captain's mistake, I made the ambassador wait halfway between the bridge and the gate aforesaid, and the captain and Francesco, with their nobles, came up from behind and welcomed the ambassador, the captain saying, " Welcome. Our Lord and the cardinals send their households to do you honor. Welcome."

The households of the cardinals were scattered in both directions, so that the ambassador could not see them at the time, but he overtook them and they each joined his train but said nothing to him.

The ambassador had only five retainers, and with him was the Lord Giorgio Bucciardo, cousin of the Bishop of Arles, also his interpreter with two servants. This Giorgio repeated the captain's words to the ambassador, and then replied in his name. The ambassador rode between the captain on his right, and the Pope's son on his left, from the aforesaid place to his place of entertainment. There also went outside the gate to meet the ambassador the lay ambassadors of the King of Poland, of the Seignory of Venice, and of the Dukes of Milan, of Florence and Siena.

During these past days I was summoned to the Lord Cardinals of Benevento and Santa Anastasia to arrange for the reception of the said relic, and I found there with them Giovanni Pietro, Lord Bishop of Urbino. Many things relative to the ceremony were spoken of, among others that on account of the ill health of our Most Holy Lord the spearhead should be conveyed by way of the meadows to the palace of the Spinelli outside of the Porta Viridarii and should be borne thence in procession by way of the aforesaid gate to the castle. This would be the most convenient route for the procession in the extreme heat of this season or in the case of mud

if the rain falls on that day as it has for many days
past.

On Sunday, the third of June, 1492, in the first
chamber beyond the hall of the Pontiffs above the
garden a low chair of gold brocade was placed ready
against the wall with one step leading up to it, and
above it a golden canopy was spread, and around the
chair on either side many velvet-covered stools were
set in preparation for the marriage of the Pope's
nephew which was to be celebrated there. As the
hour drew near at about two in the afternoon, the
Cardinals of Benevento and Santa Anastasia according to the instructions of our Most Holy Lord went
to the Prince of Capua and escorted him between
them from his apartments into the presence of the
Pontiff who was accompanied by his princes and
barons. When he had come to the Pontiff, the ladies
were awaited, and after their coming the Pontiff
came out to the chamber aforesaid and took his
seat upon the said chair.

On his right were the Lord Cardinals of San Pietro
in Vincoli and Santa Anastasia, on his left Benevento,
and next to him the Prince of Capua. Next to
Santa Anastasia with a moderate space between upon
similar stools sat Teodorina, the Pope's daughter,
and Peretta, her daughter, Battistina, the bride, also
her daughter Maddalena, the daughter of the late
Lorenzo de' Medici, wife of the Pope's son, and many
ladies after her. Next to the Prince of Capua, that

is to say, on the left of the Pope, stood Aloysio of
Aragon, Marquis of Gerace, the bridegroom, the
Duke of Amalfi, Francesco Cibo, the Pope's son, and
many other nobles to the number of about forty.
After silence had been secured, the Reverend Lord
Giovanni, Archbishop of Ragusa, the Datary, kneeling before our Most Holy Lord at a proper distance
of two cannes or thereabouts made a brief oration in
which he expounded the institution of the sacrament
of matrimony and its dignity.

Thereupon he rose and stood in the same place,
and turning to the Illustrious Lord Alfonso of
Aragon, the half-brother of the Prince of Capua,
spoke these or similar words: " Most Illustrious Lord
Luigi of Aragon, will you take the most Illustrious
Lady Battistina Cibo, here present, to be your lawful
spouse and wife? ".   And he straightway replied, " I
will."   Then, turning to Battistina, the archbishop
said: " Most Illustrious Lady, will you take the Most
Illustrious Lord Luigi of Aragon, here present, to be
your lawful spouse and husband? "   To these words
she made no reply, but after the archbishop had repeated the words, she replied, " I will."   The bride
and bridegroom then approached the Pontiff, and
kneeling before him, the bridegroom placed the wed-
ding-ring upon the third finger of the bride's left
hand, and then many rings upon the other fingers of
that hand, and upon the other, the right hand of the
bride, which Giovanni Fontano, the chief secretary

of the Most Serene King of Naples, extended to him. Next, the bridegroom first and then the bride kissed the Pope's foot, and the bridegroom arose and kissed the bride. She then returned to her place, and the bridegroom sat beside her. The Pontiff then rose and returned to his apartment, and all the others separated and went their own ways.

On Thursday, the 14th of June, 1492, at about seven in the evening, the Reverend Father in Christ, John, Lord Bishop of Durham, ambassador of the King of England, entered the city by the Porta Viridarii. He was received by the household of the Pope and those of all the cardinals and by those princes who were then in the city, and was escorted by them in the usual order to the house of the late Giacomo Biqueto which was prepared as his residence. There was a dispute between the ambassadors of the King of Spain, the Bishops of Beja and Astorga on the one hand, and the Lord Giovanni Gilio of Lucca, formerly ambassador of the king of England, on the other, upon the question of precedence, and I was persuaded by the said bishops to give a seat on the right of the Bishop of Durham to Giovanni, Archbishop of Ragusa, the first of the palace clergy, and that on his left to the aforesaid Lord Giovanni Gilio.

On the following day the Pope fell ill, and through fear of his death Prospero Colonna and Giovanni Jordano, son of Vergineo Ursino, who were staying with the Cardinal of San Pietro in Vincoli, came with many other barons and Roman citizens to the palace of the conservators, and stated and made known to the said officials and citizens that they, the barons, were of one mind with the Roman people whom they dearly loved, and forthwith they offered themselves and their castles and their goods to the Roman people for their welfare and goodwill, and asked them, if the death of the Pontiff should chance to come, that they would join with them for their aid; on their part the conservators and citizens offered them whatever could be offered.

On the 25th of July, 1492, St. James' day, about six or seven o'clock in the morning, Pope Innocent VIII died. May his soul rest in peace!

# V

## THE ACCESSION OF ALEXANDER VI

IN the year of the Lord 1492, on Saturday, the 11th of August, at noon, Roderigo Borgia, vice-chancellor and the nephew of Calixtus III, was created Pope and named Alexander VI.

On the 27th of August Alexander was crowned in St. Peter's. Then he went in the customary manner to the Church of St. John Lateran while the greatest honor was done to him throughout the city by the Roman people with triumphal arches and with more than there was ever done to other Popes.

And in the first consistory he held, he created the Archbishop of Mount Royal, his nephew from a sister, a cardinal.

After his coronation it was brought to his knowledge that from the day of the last illness of Innocent until his coronation more than two hundred and twenty men had been assassinated in various places and at various times. It was also brought to his knowledge who the murderers were and the reasons and success they had had. Of all this that had gone on in Rome he received full knowledge.

On the 3d of September of the year 1492 Salva-

tor, the son of Tutio del Rosso, insulted Domenico
Beneacceduto, his enemy, on the Campo dei Fiori,
with whom he was under a pledge of five hundred
ducats to keep the peace. He stabbed him twice
with a dagger, inflicting a mortal wound of which
he died forthwith. On the 4th the pope dispatched
his vice-chamberlain with the magistrates who proceeded thither attended by a throng to destroy his
house, which was done. On the same day the
brother of the aforesaid Salvator, one Hieronymus,
was hanged on the instigation of Domenico. Thus
assuredly by the will of God, on a single day justice
was accomplished. The fine was collected from the
guarantors by the Pope.

In the same month Alexander appointed prison
inspectors in addition to four commissaries to hear
complaints in Rome. Furthermore he appointed his
officials for the administration of Vignola, fixed an
audience for Wednesday for all citizens, men as well
as women, received the complaints himself and began
to administer justice in an admirable way.

On Monday, the 10th of December, 1492, I rode
at daybreak to Marino to instruct the noble Lord
Federigo of Aragon, Prince of Altamura, second son
of King Ferdinand of Sicily and Jerusalem, with regard to the ceremonies at his reception before his
arrival in Rome. The royal ambassador in Rome,
Giacomo Pontano, who declared that he had received
a special letter about this matter from his master,

had asked for me the evening before at about eleven o'clock. I found there the prince whom I instructed in detail with reference to the order and arrangement of the entry and reception as well as of his own demeanor.

On Tuesday, the 11th of December, 1492, about two o'clock in the afternoon the cardinals Carafa and Piccolomini went out beyond the second milestone before Rome in order to meet the prince as their special friend. They greeted him with the usual honors and he rode then between them until they came to the road that leads through the Porta Latina, where the cardinals took leave of him. The prince continued on his way with his suite until he reached the Church of St. John Lateran and its main portal, firstly, in order to avoid the mud, and then because two cardinals who were to meet him at the gate of St. John Lateran had not yet arrived.

In the meantime the suites of all the cardinals and princely ambassadors in Rome came to meet him; further, one after the other, Giulio Orsini, the brother of Cardinal Orsini, Gerardo Usodimare, Domenico Doria and other noblemen who dismounted from their horses and were for making obeisance to the prince. He did not allow it, however, until they had remounted their horses. The prince waited about an hour before the portal of the aforementioned basilica for the arrival of the two cardinals who had been despatched and who arrived finally after six o'clock, namely Juan Borgia and Ascanio Sforza. They received him in the usual way and escorted him in their midst.

After the arrival at the place of San Giovanni in Laterano where one sees the bronze statue of a horseman there came the prelates of the palace with the suite of the Pope which also greeted the prince in the usual way, although the major-domo of the Apostolic palace, Bartolommeo Marti, had made his speech as a prelate. Together with the prince seven other ambassadors had been sent to swear the oath of loyalty to the Pope. I assigned every one his place in due order of precedence and in this order we rode straight on passing to the right of the coliseum to Santa Maria Nuova, along by the Hospital of the Consolation and the house of the Savelli, through the Peschiera, the square of the Jews, the dei Fiore meadows to the Apostolic palace near St. Peter's. I assume that the reason that the cardinals were so late was that the Pope endeavored in this way to prevent the prince from continuing on the same day to the palace and to divert him to the inn Ad Apostolos where he was supposed to take his quarters. Behind the barons, nobles and the whole retinue of the prince rode the shield-bearers of the Pope and our barons with the captain of the palace. There were two pages before the armed men of the prince and six before those of the Pope: The first with cross-bow and quiver of gilded silver in French

dress and on a French horse, the second in Turkish
dress on a Berber horse, the third clad in Spanish
fashion with a long lance on a small Spanish hack,
the fourth with the rain-coat of his master, the fifth
with a valise of a crimson color, the sixth with a
sword sheathed in its scabbard with a handle studded
with pearls and precious stones estimated at six
thousand ducats in value.   There were several rid-
ers mounted on very magnificent horses, dressed in
gold brocade and wearing jewels of great value on
their breasts and in their hats and barrets.   The
prince wore a garment of violet velvet, a chain of
pearls and jewels, worth six thousand ducats, and
a belt with a sword of the same value.   His bridle
was studded all over with pearls and precious stones,
worth three thousand ducats, and the whole harness
was gilded before and behind.

The suite was preceded by two hundred sumpters
all covered with red cloth and the whole suite included seven or eight hundred people as I was told.
When we passed through a somewhat narrow alley,
Cardinal Juan Borgia rode first, followed by the
prince, and after him came Ascanio Sforza, which
was improper.   The other two Cardinals, Carafa
and Piccolomini, behaved differently, for in the same
alley they stayed behind him, which was more
proper.

Having arrived at the palace they went up to the
Pope who awaited the prince in the last of the nine

chambers besides the secret chamber. Five cardinals were with him, namely Carafa, Domenico delle
Rovere, Antoniotto Gentile Pallavicini, the Chamberlain Orsini and Piccolomini. After the prince
there entered the aforementioned ambassadors and
all barons and nobles of the suite of the prince.
After Federigo had been permitted by the Pope to
kiss his foot, his hand and his mouth, they too kissed
the foot of the Pope while the prince was kneeling
on a cushion at the left of the Pope. For the Cardinal Ascanio Sforza had decided that the prince
should be allowed to sit down only after all of the
cardinals had taken their seats, while I more cautiously preferred that he should wait kneeling there
instead of taking a seat that was not proper for
him. For he should have had a seat after the last
deacon-cardinal if not further to the front and before most of the deacons. Sforza, however, wanted
to place him even behind the cardinals in order to
favor his own duke of Milan.

After this reception the prince, accompanied by
Carafa and Piccolomini, rode to the inn Ad Apostolos and to the palace of Cardinal Giuliano delle
Rovere where he was to take up his quarters. After
him came the prelates of the palace, the ambassadors, and the other prelates in the same order as
they had come from the Lateran church to the Apostolic palace. Before the portal of the palace the
prince was about to take leave of the cardinals with

thanks but they accompanied him still farther to the entrance of the garden where they stopped. Only at that point did they part from him and without being able to thank he could not express his thanks to every one in the accustomed manner because it was night and because they had accompanied him there contrary to the rules of precedence.

We went from the Vatican to the inn Ad Apostolos through the Via Del Papa. The numerous drivers of the sumpters did not come to the Apostolic palace first but they went by the aforementioned way to the bridge of San Angelo, keeping on this side of the river, and turned later to the right towards the palace of the Cardinal of Parma, Sclafenata, and thence straight on to Ad Apostolos.

Before the Pope left his chamber this morning, the 21st of December, he called together all the cardinals and sent for us two clerks of the ceremonies, Giovanni Maria de Podio and myself, to inquire what measures were to be taken to-day for the reception of Federigo of Aragon, who was to swear the oath of loyalty that day at the consistory and what place was to be assigned to him among the cardinals or behind them. I replied to his Holiness:

When Francesco of Aragon came to swear allegiance to Pope Innocent VIII of blessed memory in the name of his royal father whose fourth son he was, two cardinals had been sent as far as the Apostolic chamber to meet him and they accompanied him from there to the Pope. The same procedure therefore might be followed this time, although not quite fittingly because such escort was not customary for those who had been sent to swear allegiance but on other occasions only for sons of kings and great princes. As for the second point the seat before the second last deacon-cardinal, namely Francesco Severino, was to be assigned to him.

The Pope added to this that Federigo had indeed, as the Governor of Rome had recalled to him, had his seat when he was in the city in the times of Paul II; before the deceased cardinal of Mantua, who then was the last deacon-cardinal. Concerning my answer the Pope asked for the opinions of the cardinals standing around him while we were kneeling down before the Pope in their midst. The cardinals Michaeli, Pallavicini, Orsini and Sforza declared expressly that as far as they could remember Francesco, the brother of Federigo, had had his seat after all the deacon-cardinals. I considered this an error but did not say anything. They objected, however, saying that Francisco had been the fourth son while Federigo was the second, and that there was therefore a great difference between the two. Ascanio Sforza asked whether Federigo or the Duke of Milan was higher in rank. I answered that according to our ceremonies Federigo was much higher in rank than the Duke for as the son of a king he had precedence not only over the Duke of Milan but

also over the electors.   Cardinal Zeno before giving
his vote remarked that this ought not to be done in
our presence.   But when the Pope answered that we
ought to hear it because it concerned our duties, he
voted that he would accept the decision of Agostino
Patrizzi, and he sent for him but he could not come
as the Cardinal Piccolomini had sent him to accompany Federigo.   Nevertheless Zeno did not want to
forestall him with his vote and declared that he
would not vote.

Finally the Pope decided on the basis of a mere
majority of votes that the two younger deacon-
cardinals should accompany Federigo to the presence of the Pope and that the seat before the last
deacon-cardinal should be assigned to him, because
he had had the same seat once before, and also because on this day he ought not to sit with the cardinals on account of swearing allegiance, but ought to
stand together with those who had been sent with
him behind the cardinal-presbyters at the usual
place.

Now when Federigo came to the palace, in order
not to lose any time, there went out to meet him as
far as the staircase of the floor of the Apostolic
chamber those assigned for his escort, the vice-chancellor Ascanio Sforza, San Severino and the two last
deacon-cardinals as well as several assistants of the
Pope.

The prince was first permitted to kiss the foot,

hand and mouth of the Pope, and after him the eight others who had been delegated with him. Then the prince submitted the credentials from his father, the King of Naples, with the remark that his illustrious father was laying himself humbly at the feet of his Holiness. Then they took up their places again while the two cardinals accompanied the prince to the end but not beyond the benches of the cardinals. Paulus de Planca made his speech and the Pope answered.

Then Cardinal Podocatoro read the royal letter which said that he, the king, sent his dearest son, the illustrious Duke of Andria, Prince of Altamura and Admiral of the Kingdom, together with all his other co-ambassadors to swear allegiance. Zeno, the bishop of San Marco, delivered the oration. The consistory ended, the prince carried the edge of the posterior end of the papal pluviale. The cardinals Piccolomini and Orsini assisted the Pope during the entire time. Also they stood up during the whole reception taking seats only afterward on their bench.

Laying off his robes the Pope ordered the cardinals Cibo and Colonna to escort the prince between them in the usual way to the inn " Ad Apostolos," which was done. Where the way narrowed down, they let the prince precede and quite correctly, for this was the proper way, even if Ascanio Sforza behaved differently with San Severino and the other day with Juan Borgia, gratifying his special mood.

Lord Federigo came to-day to the palace in great magnificence with his whole retinue, three pages in German dress, crimson colored and adorned with gorgeous pearls and jewels riding before on horses that had been bridled in the German way.

During the previous days the several cardinals had made their calls upon Federigo which he answered to-day and on the following days. It would have been more proper, of course, if the calls had been made and returned after allegiance had been sworn, but since Carafa and Piccolomini as personal friends of the prince, as I believe, had called on him immediately after his arrival and together with them Rovere, Cibo and Colonna, they all succumbed to the same mistake.

On Monday, the 24th of December, the day before Christmas, the Pope who had been adorned with the usual robes in the third of the new chambers, went through the two halls, the new one and the large old one, and down the stairs into the court where the cardinals usually dismount from their horses. From there he proceeded by way of the Basilica to St. Peter, the cardinals going before in their usual dress and the suite of prelates also in their customary coats. In the Basilica the cardinals and prelates after having made their obeisance put on their robes in unseemly disorder and without waiting until all had completed the obeisance, for only then were they supposed to robe themselves as were those of the elder deacons who were to assist them.

At the request of the Pope our sacristan had hung old Greek paintings around below the tribune on three sides above the main altar of the Basilica, as was the custom in the times of Paul II. Two large crystal lamps were also hung at the entrance.

After the vespers were ended the Pope was borne back in the customary way to the palace passing through the old halls to the Camera Papagalli, where he laid off the blessed garments and assigned the new chambers to the prince to retire there for the night. The chambers were adorned magnificently, the third, fourth and fifth being hung with Alexandrine velvet in cerulean blue with curtains of gold brocade while in the second chamber stood the bed of crimson colored velvet.

The 27th of December, 1492.— About ten days ago the news came from Barcelona that King Ferdinand of Spain had been severely wounded in his neck by a peasant on the steps of his palace on the 7th of December, so that six stitches had to be applied. The criminal had received two wounds from the men of the King and had been seized. A few days later the additional news arrived that the King was out of danger and that the peasant had acted under a vision from the devil. The devil had appeared to him twenty years ago in the form of an angel and had commanded him to kill the King in order to become king himself, but he had forbidden him to tell anybody of this. After that he had appeared to him again and again urging him on. The peasant had been forced to a confession by the promise of reward. Then the scales fell from his eyes as it were, and he had repented immediately from the depth of his heart and considered himself worthy of the most cruel death. Whereupon he was condemned to be executed after the following manner, namely, that all his limbs or extremities of every limb should be cut off one after the other and at intervals of time but on one and the same day. In order, however, that he should not be driven to despair he was given at the beginning a heavy blow on the head by order of the queen so that he might die more quickly and would suffer less while his limbs were being cut off by his consciousness being dimmed.

All this was made known to the Pope on the 27th of December through a royal letter that was brought to him by the bishops of Bajadoz and Astorga as ambassadors. The Pope decided to have a mass said in honor of the glorious Virgin Mary for the recovery of the King on Saturday, the 29th of December, in the chapel of Maria delle Febbri besides the Basilica of St. Peter. Afterwards the face of Our Lord and the spear should be shown to the people and the day should be celebrated as a feast

day by all craftsmen and others. And he ordered
that all this ought to be proclaimed in public and he
made known through placards in the various quarters of the city.

# VI

## THE CORONATION OF THE KING OF NAPLES

FOR the carnival (1493) nine prizes in the races were offered, three as usual on the first Sunday of Lent for Berber horses, steeds and horses, the six others for the Jews, the boys, the young men and the old men, the donkeys and the buffaloes, as it had been done in former years and was customary.

On Wednesday, the 27th of February, 1493, the Pope heard mass in his own chamber and decided thereupon that he would go to Santa Maria Maggiore where he would first hold a short consistory and then after a prayer at the altar would examine how far the construction of the church, that is to say of the canopy of the altar, had advanced. He asked me whether it was right to pronounce the benediction to the people after the prayer. I answered no, and that it was an extraordinary procedure because nothing, neither mass nor vespers, should precede the benediction. I further explained to his Holiness that there was a good and regular rule that the Pope should ride without a mitre, the cardinals to follow him. Also it would not be quite

proper that the Pope should ride during Lent in a
white cowl and an adorned surplice, but rather in a
red cowl and a violet surplice.  He answered that
he had decided that the cardinals should ride before
him and not after him, also that he intended to wear
a white and not a red cowl and not a violet surplice
but a gorgeous one adorned with pearls.  According to his decision he was adorned in his private
chamber and went then to the Camera Papagalli,
where he held a consistory of one hour's duration.
Then he mounted a white horse covered with cloth
and adorned with crimson velvet.  Preceded by the
cross and the cardinals and followed as usual by the
privy chamberlains, the assistants and prelates, he
went through the Campo dei Fiori and the Square
of the Jews and passed the house of Cardinal Savelli, the church of Santa Maria de Consolazione and
St. Adrian and went then to Santa Maria Maggiore where he was received at the portal by the
clergy in procession.

The arch priest of the Basilica, Cardinal Savelli,
gave him the cross to kiss and the clergy sang:
*Ecce sacerdos magnus,* etc.  The Pope pronounced
a prayer on the folding-chair before the altar and
then stepped up to the altar and kissed it, deposit-
ing thereon ten gold ducats as I had reminded him
to do.  Then, turning to the crowd, he blessed the
people as he had decided to do.  During the ceremony the cross was held lower than is the custom in

St. Peter's. Then he went up to the palace saying a prayer before the image of the Virgin Mary and the picture of St. Luke. He inspected the work that had been done, returning afterward to the Basilica. Then he went home on horseback, passing St. Basilius and San Marco, through the Via Polliciaria near the Casa Massimi and the palace of Cardinal Carafa, and thence through the Parione Square to the palace.

An extraordinarily large number of armed men took part in this mounted procession which was not exactly approved by everybody. For our procession, that is to say, the baggage of the cardinals, was preceded by several crossbow-bearers and bands of soldiers and in the same way several men with lances and in full armor followed, the prelates riding behind the Pope. The governor of the city with the magistrates and a few of the district-wardens and the Bargello [1] and many men on horseback and on foot presented themselves to the Pope at various corners and places. He ordered therefore that the captains of the Church and of the portal of the palace should proceed between him and the cardinals, and that the Lords of Sermoneta and Corrigia and many other leaders of the soldiers should follow him after the physicians and before the assisting prelates, as was done while they passed over the whole square of St. Peter as far as about the house of

[1] The chief of police.

Cardinal Soderini. When I noticed the inverted order, I told the Pope that this would be quite unseemly and tried to persuade him to permit me to assign them their places. He answered me I should arrange them before the captains and after all the cardinals. But when he heard that this would be most objectionable to the cardinals, he ordered me to place them before the cross after the armed men on foot who marched along in quite extraordinary large numbers with long lances, bare swords, crossbows and other arms. This I did.

On the 10th of June, 1493, Alexander, the son of the Lord of Pesaro, arrived in Rome with a large suite of bishops, and on the very day of his arrival was bethrothed to the illegitimate daughter of Pope Alexander. While still a cardinal, the Pope had married her to a Spaniard. As Pope, however, he wished to improve the position of his daughter and therefore dissolved the marriage, bestowing three thousand ducats upon the Spaniard as compensation. Now he married her to the aforementioned Lord,[1] while her first husband was still living, but the latter kept his mouth shut on account of the money and yielded.

On Wednesday, the 7th of May, 1494, a marriage was contracted between Gofredo Borgia, son of Alexander VI, and Sancia of Aragon, the illegitimate daughter of King Alphonso II of Sicily.

[1] His real name was Giovanni Sforza.

On Thursday, the 8th of May, 1494, the day of
the Ascension and the feast of the Apparition of the
Archangel Michael, on which day the coronation of
King Alphonso was to be held, I went before daybreak into the cathedral of Naples and made all
necessary preparations.   In the early morning there
was a violent storm and a heavy fall of rain which
ceased, however, when the coronation started and
was succeeded by the most beautiful weather all day
long and also during the following day.   From the
royal treasure chamber were brought first, the royal
crown in a vessel of gilded silver.   The crown was
adorned with pearls and precious stones and lined
with a cap of white damask from which hung down
two silken ribbons that were brought together beneath the chin with a button,— for the King did not
wear another cap under the crown.   Then the sword
was brought in its scabbard, studded with pearls and
precious stones from the end to end, then the silver
scepter with a gilded lily at the upper end, about
two and a half spans long and somewhat thinner
than my little finger.   Then came the round gilded
imperial globe at the top of which stood a small
gilded cross of silver while beneath there was a metal
ring with a silken cord so that the globe could be
fastened to the left finger of the king in order that
it might not fall from his hand.   All that I placed
on the altar, one beside the other.   When the legate
*in pontificalibus* took his seat upon his folding-chair

before the altar in the middle he was approached by order of the King by his secretary, Giovanni Pontano, and another who stated that the kings of Aragon did not usually kneel down while they were receiving the royal insignia, also that it was not the custom that they swore or read personally the oath during their coronation and installation, but that some one else did this in their name. Only after the oath had been read would they swear it themselves on their knees. Although they had heard from me that the King had to kneel down during the swearing in and had to read personally, Pontano was for reading the oath in the presence of the King as he was seated, whereupon the King would rise, kneel down on a cushion, and with his hand on the Evangiles would swear to keep what had been read.

The legate called me nearer and I said that the procedure ought not to be in any case as suggested but that it was customary that the one who kneeled down should swear his oath into the hands of the legate as the deputy of the Holy Roman Church, the Apostolic See and His Holiness, the Pope, and that the King had to swear it himself. The legate agreed with me. In order not to appear completely unsuccessful in their endeavors, Pontano and the other secretary asked the legate to grant that the King should at least kneel down on a cushion and that the secretary should read before the King from the book and that the King should repeat it. This was per-

mitted by the legate because we explained that it
would not be in contraction with the usual ceremonies
and that it only required more time.

About eleven o'clock, while it was still raining,
the King appeared in the church with his courtiers
and barons.   He wore over a close-fitting garment
of black satin a larger one of crimson colored brocade, lined with flounces of ermine and with this a
barret with a pendant of three pearls and one precious stone worth about ten thousand ducats.   He
kept the barret on his head until he received the
crown.   He proceeded as far as the middle of the
choir of the canons.   There the Archbishop of
Naples and the Patriarch of Antiochia came forward
to meet him.   They saluted and escorted him, the
prelates rising to salute him while the King himself
made a bow and then he took his seat.

After the bull had been read by Stephanus de
Narnia the King knelt down on a cushion before
the legate.   At his left knelt his secretary, Giovanni
Pontano, who held in writing in his hands the oath
to be sworn by the King and read it.   King Alphonso
repeated it word for word.   After he had spoken the
words, *Et haec sancta Dei evangelia,* the legate took
the opened missal and held it so on his knees that he
had the image of the Crucified at his right before
him.   At the left side I had had laid a chart with
the beginning words of the four Evangiles.   The
King then laid his right hand on the Evangiles and

his left on the Crucified and swore the oath. Thereupon the legate invested the King by handing him
over the banner and introduced him into its possession with the words: " By virtue of Apostolic author-
ity." There had been a long discussion about these
words the day before.

After having been invested the King handed the
banner over to the chancellor of the kingdom, who
stood prepared to receive it, between his two assisting prelates. The notary Stephauus de Narnia
called upon those standing around to be witnesses
of the investiture, but the treasurer of the King said
nothing. When the legate, in reading the litany,
came to the royal blessing, he pronounced twice by
inattention in the tune of the litany: *ut hunc electum
in regem coronadum benedicere dignetur.* He repeated, therefore, and added at the third time: *et
consecrare.* All prayers, and so forth, were read by
the legate with the proper voice.

While the legate after the blessing of the King,
was confessing with his assistants, the deacon and
subdeacon, the King knelt before his folding-chair
turning with the footstool toward the corner of the
Evangiles of the altar. He confessed with his two
chief chaplains and remained on his knees until the
legate had censed the altar and read near his folding-
chair the introitus and the epistle and had sat down
— an arrangement I had made in order to be able
to be of greater assistance to the King.

After having made a bow the King then entered
the sacristy where the Apostolic Subdeacon Ber-
nardius Gambara dried his arms and shoulders.[1]
Before this he had laid down the long garment which
the legate considered as a perquisite that was by custom due to him as he had performed the consecra-
tion.   He had told me, therefore, when he sat down
in his folding-chair after the introitus and the *Kyrie
Eleison* and before I led the King to the sacristy,
that I should have it brought to him.

The King was then dressed with another garment
of black satin with a long outer garment reaching
down to the floor of the crimson-colored satin with
narrow sleeves, then with sandals and shoes over the
black stockings, and with everything else as it had
been arranged according to the program.   The black
barret he kept on and advanced thus to the throne.
There he spoke the introitus and the rest kneeling
down before the throne together with his chief chaplains.

In the meantime the legate spoke the *Pax vobis*
turning to the altar through the inattention of himself and his associates.   Before the King left the
sacristy, he sent out one of his pages with the aforementioned garment of brocade in order that I should
hand it over to the legate who accepted it grate-
fully.   As a matter of fact this garment and the
small one of black satin which the King had on was

1 The King has been anointed.

due to me as a gift. But out of modesty I did not ask for the small one and did not want to resist the request of the legate. He also told me to have presented to him as a due gift the barret of the King with the pendant. I answered that it would certainly be modest if I requested it for myself, but that if he insisted, I would do as he wished. I did not do so, however.

The King was then crowned in the proper order and the royal insignia were handed over to him as aforementioned. But neither during this ceremony nor before during the anointment could all the prelates form the prescribed circle behind the King on account of the great throng of people composing the royal and princely suites, the barons, courtiers, and ambassadors, who crowded the prelates by pushing forward.

After the coronation the King stepped up to the seat of the throne and sat down while the populace cheered repeatedly shouting: *Viva re Alphonso!*

# VII

## KING CHARLES VIII IN ROME

ON the 10th of December, 1494, the ambassadors of the King of France who had repeatedly
demanded an open letter from the Pope during these
days in regard to the passage through his territory
and concerning supplies, again made representations
to his Holiness on this matter. The Pope replied
to them after the consistory that in no case would
he grant free passage and supplies to the King and
that they could inform the King of this according to
their pleasure.

On Thursday, the 18th of December, all the possessions of the Pope were packed up for departure
with the exception of the bed and the ordinary sideboard. In addition the paraments of the sacristy
of the Apostolic chapel and the whole furnishings of
the palace and other papal belongings were sent to
the castle San Angelo. All the cardinals were prepared for departure with freshly shod horses and
mules in readiness.

In former days as well as at this time, that is,
on the 19th, 21st, 22nd and 23rd of December, the
men of the French King organized raids over the

Monte Mario as far as San Lazaro and the adjoining
meadow of San Angelo. They also decided to fall
upon the city by stealth on one of these nights, the
French through one gate and the Colonnese through
the other. For aid and assistance a thousand
Frenchmen were to come up by ship from Ostia.
But the wind rose so strongly against them that
they could not complete their program. Otherwise
they would have carried their evil designs and
broken into the city through the Porta San Paolo,
setting fire, pillaging and doing much mischief.
Some pointed out as the author of this plan the
Cardinal de Gurck who had come, as the report went,
in his own person to the vicinity of the city gate
during that night, but had withdrawn again as the
result of the adverse wind.

In any case he was the main cause for the advance
of the King against Rome. For he had caused the
inhabitants of Aquapendente and of other lands of
the Church to admit the King of France by praising
to the skies the honesty and worth of himself and
his men with the assurance that they would pay in
full and in coin for every fowl and every egg or even
for the smallest trifle. He asserted also the Pope
himself had promised him access to and passage
through the lands of the Church. In this way he
induced the population to let in the King and his
men against the decided will of the Pope. And in
order to win over also the curials of German nation-

ality he wrote an open letter which he had sent to us who were most prominent.

On Friday, the 26th of December, 1494, on the feast of St. Stephen, the first martyr, Cardinal Cibo, celebrated the solemn mass in the main chapel of the palace in the presence of the Pope. After the Pope had entered there came also three ambassadors of the King of France, who had arrived during the night before, namely the grand-marshal of France, Jean de Ganay, first president of the Parliament of Paris, and a third one, all laymen. To the first I assigned a seat on the steps of the throne before and above the senator, the two others were assigned to the bench of the lay ambassadors, where there were seated already two ambassadors of the King of Naples. These would not have anything to do with the newcomers, explaining that they were not aware that they were ambassadors, and they left their seats. By special order of the Pope I informed them that those were ambassadors of the King of France, whereupon they yielded and returned to their seats. Many Frenchmen had appeared with the three ambassadors, a large number of whom pushed themselves forward without any consideration near the prelates and sat down on their benches. When I showed them away and assigned them to their proper seats, the Pope summoned me and said angrily that I had ruined his intentions, and that I should permit the Frenchmen to remain where they wanted to. I replied to his Holiness that for God's sake he should not get excited as I now knew his intentions, and would not say anything more to them wherever they should stand. On Wednesday, the 31st of December, 1494, I rode out by order of the Pope quite early in the morning to meet the King of France in order to explain to him the arrangements of the reception according to the ceremonial and to receive his decision and carry out his Majesty's orders.

Near Galera, after two miles' journey, we met the Cardinals Giuliano delle Rovere, Gurck and Savelli, to whom I made obeisance without dismounting from my horse. Soon afterwards came the King, to whom we also made our obeisance without dismounting on account of the dirt and the rain as well as his fast approach. The Bishop of Nepi executed the commission with which he had been charged by the Pope concerning the reception of the King, and I also explained to his Majesty what I had been charged with by the Pope. The King replied he wished to come to Rome without any display whatever. I received his answer and after me Hieronymus Porcarius, in the name of the Roman authorities, placed the citizens and their possessions at the disposal of the King. The King replied in a few words without entering into this matter. The Romans withdrew and the King called me at his side, and conversed with me for about four miles continuously, asking me about the ceremonies, the condition of the Pope, the

rank and position of Cesare Borgia, and a number
of other things, so that I found it almost impossible
to give proper answers to every particular question.

Near Borghetto two ambassadors of Venice came
to meet the King. They dismounted and kissed their
own hands before they offered them to the King.
They did not kiss the hand of the King, however.
Behind them came Cardinal Sforza, who greeted the
King bareheaded without dismounting from his mule.
The King too bared his head and greeted the cardinal. Then they covered their heads and Sforza,
riding at the left of the King, escorted him into
the city over the Ponte Molle as far as the Palace
San Marco, the usual residence of the Cardinal Cibo.
The whole way to the palace was one mud and puddle.
In all the streets from the palace of the Cardinal
Costa near the Church San Lorenzo in Luzina as
far as San Marco there was an illumination of fires
and torches at eleven o'clock in the evening and all
shouted: *Francia! Francia! Colonna! Colonna! Vincula! Vincula!* When we had arrived before the
Palace San Marco, Cardinal Sforza did not dismount from his mule but baring his head took leave
from the King, with his permission, before he entered the portal. Nor did delle Rovere nor any
other of the cardinals accompany the King. To-
day before the entry of the King into Rome the
keys to the gates of the Viridarii, of Belvedere, of
the middle gate and of all other gates of the city

were entrusted to the grand-marshal of France, the above-mentioned ambassador of the King, upon his request and with the consent of the Pope. For the Frenchmen said — and this was true — that the keys had been surrendered the other day to the Duke of Calabria when he was in Rome and that the King of France was not inferior to him.

On Monday, the 12th of January, 1495, the King sights. He was accompanied only by the Cardinal of France rode alone through the city to see the of St. Denis, Jean de Villiers de la Groslaye, who rode with a few nobles at a distance behind the King. Between him and the King there rode a captain of the body-guard that marched with the King looking after the men as they marched along. The cardinal followed them with the other nobles.

On Thursday, the 29th of January, 1495, there arrived from France 18,000 ducats in barrels on mules for the French King and on the next day 4000 more were brought for the expenses that the King and those with him had every day.

On Friday, the 30th of January, 1495, it was reported to the Pope that Cesare had fled from Velletri in the disguise of a royal groom. He had left the King already before arriving there and had slept during that night in the house of the auditor of the Rota, Antonio Flores. When he departed together with the King, Cesare had taken along with him from Rome quite openly nineteen sumpters with his baggage under precious covers, amongst these two which were laden with his vessels of credence.

These remained behind already on the first day while the King and the cardinal were riding to Marino, and returned in the evening to Rome. The servants of the cardinal pretended at the court that the sumpters had been robbed and pillaged. The other seventeen went to the court of the King, who confiscated them after the flight of the cardinal. When he had the bales opened, there was nothing in them. This has been told to me, but I think it is a lie.

On Wednesday, the 25th of February, 1495, Djem, alias Zizim,[1] brother of the Grand Turk, whom his Holiness had surrendered recently by reason of a treaty with the King, died in Naples, that is to say, in Castro Capuano, through eating or drinking something disagreeable to which his stomach was not accustomed. His corpse was then sent to the Grand Turk at his urgent request together with all the household of the deceased. The Grand Turk is said to have paid or given a large sum of money on this account, and to have received this household with favor.

On the 15th of March, 1495, the Neapolitan Castell dell' Ovo surrendered to the King of France.

[1] See Appendix.

Performances were given before him by his men with
French humor of tragedies and comedies representing
the Pope, the King of Spain and the Doges of Venice
as concluding a league and alliance with each other.

# VIII

## ALEXANDER AND HIS FAMILY

ON Friday, the 20th of May, 1496, at six o'clock in the afternoon an entry was made into Rome through the Lateran gate by one Gofredo Borgia of Aragon, a son of the Pope, about fourteen years old and his wife, Sancia of Aragon, with about six ladies of her household. There went out to meet them the captain of the squadron with his men-at-arms, about two hundred of them, the suites of all the cardinals and the papal prelates. For every single cardinal had been requested that morning by papal runners at the instigation of Cesare to send their chaplains and men-at-arms to meet his brother Gofredo, upon his entry into the city. This they all did and dispatched their men as far as beyond the aforementioned gate, and here Lucretia Sforza, also a daughter of the Pope, and wife of Giovanni Sforza, Lord of Pesaro and sister of Gofredo met them with twelve other women. Two pages preceded her bearing two cloaks and riding on two horses one of which was covered with precious gold brocade, the other with crimson velvet. She greeted her brother and his wife with affection.

When we had come to the palace, the Pope went
to the hall of the Pontiffs and sat down on an elevated seat that had been prepared for him there in
the center of the left wall with a green carpet before
it on which was depicted the Savior laying His
fingers on the side of St. Thomas. Another similar
carpet was laid over the seat. Eleven cardinals
were standing around in their coats. We entered
the hall through the three ordinary halls, the chamber of paraments, the Camera Papagalli and the
others. Before the footstool of the Pope there stood
a small stool on which lay a cushion of brocade, and
before it four larger cushions of crimson velvet cross-
wise on the floor. Gofredo made obeisance to the
Pope in the customary way and kissed his foot and
hand. The Pope took the head of Gofredo between
both his hands bowing his head over him but without
kissing him. There followed Sancia, who in the same
way kissed the foot and hand of the Pope and whose
head he took in the same way between his hands.
Also Lucretia was thus received by the Pope. After
this Gofredo approached every cardinal beginning
with Pallavicini and kissed their hands, whereupon
each of them gave him a kiss upon the mouth.
Sancia too kissed the hands of the cardinals and
these took her head between their hands as if they
wanted to kiss it. During this the daughter of the
Pope stood before her father. Then Gofredo placed
himself between the cardinals Sanseverino and Cesare

Borgia, his brother.  Lucretia sat down on a cushion
on the floor at the right of the Pope, Sancia on
another one at the left of the Pope, and the other
ladies approached to kiss the papal foot.  The Pope,
Sancia and Lucretia exchanged together a few hilari-
ous remarks.

After this Gofredo, Sancia, and Lucretia and all
the others went away while the Pope remained in the
hall, and in the same order as we had come we rode
to the house of the former Cardinal della Porta,
where Gofredo and Sancia found quarters and reception.  At the entrance they thanked those who
had escorted them in the proper way; then Gofredo,
Sancia, and Lucretia entered, where they were greeted
by many Roman ladies who were awaiting them
there.

On Whitsunday, the 22nd of May, 1495, the
Pope went to St. Peter's under the mitre without
the canopy and there Cardinal Cibo celebrated
solemn mass in his presence.  The sermon was
preached by a Spaniard, a chaplain of the Bishop
of Segorbe, who was rather wordy and wearisome, to
the disgust of the Pope and all the others.  He announced a full indulgence which the Pope granted
from the beginning of the mass until he should be
carried out again from the church.  Lucretia and
Sancia were standing on the marble staircase, on
which the canonics usually sing the epistle and the
Evangile, as well as many other ladies, and they

occupied the whole stairway and the floor around it which aroused great disgust and scandal among us and the populace.

On Wednesday, the 14th of June, 1497, Cesare Borgia and Juan Borgia, Duke of Aragon, the Captain General of the guards, the favorite sons of the Pope, dined at the house of Donna Vanozza, their mother, who lived in the neighborhood of the Church of Saint Peter in Chains. Their mother and various other people were present at the dinner. After the meal, when night had fallen, Cesare urged his brother to return to the Apostolic palace. And so they both mounted the horses or mules with a few attendants, as they had not many servants with them, and rode together until they approached the neighborhood of the palace of the Vice-chancellor Ascanio Sforza, which the Pope had erected and usually occupied during his tenure of the office of Vice-chancellor.

At this point the duke declared that he would like to find entertainment somewhere and took leave of his brother, the Cardinal. He dismissed all his servants except one and retained further a masked man who had already presented himself before the dinner and had visited him in the Apostolic palace almost every day for a month. The duke took him up behind him on his mule and rode to the Square of the Jews, where he dismissed the one groom and sent him back to the palace. He instructed him, however, that he should wait for him about eight o'clock in the square, and if he had not appeared at the end of an hour he should return to the palace. Thereupon the duke departed from the groom with the masked man behind him on the back of the mule and rode no one knows whither and was murdered.

The corpse was thrown into the river at the point besides the fountain where the refuse of the streets is usually dumped into the water, near or beside the Hospital of Saint Hieronymus of the Slavonians on the road which runs from the Angel's Bridge straight to the Church of Santa Maria del Popolo. The groom who had been dismissed on the Square of the Jews was hurt seriously and wounded unto death. He was mercifully taken into the house of some one unknown to me and cared for. Unconscious as he was he could tell nothing about his instructions and the expedition of his master.

When the duke did not return to the palace on the next morning, which was Thursday, the 15th of June, his trusted servants became uneasy and one of them carried to the Pope the news of the late expedition of the duke and Cesare and the vain watch for the return of the former. The Pope was much disturbed at the news, but tried to persuade himself that the duke was enjoying himself somewhere with a girl and was embarrassed for that reason at leaving her house in broad daylight, and he clung to the hope that he might return at any rate in the evening. When this hope was not fulfilled, the Pope was stricken with deadly terror and set on foot all possible inquiries through a few of his trusted men.

Among those who were questioned was a Slavonian dealer in wood by the name of Georgio, who had unloaded his wood on the bank of the Tiber near the above-mentioned fountain and who had spent the night on his boat guarding his wood to prevent it being stolen. The question was put to him whether he had seen anything thrown into the river during the middle of the night just past, to which he made answer that at about two o'clock in the morning two men came out of a lane by the hospital on to the public road along the river. They looked about cautiously to see whether any one was passing and when they did not see anybody they disappeared again in the lane. After a little while two others came out of the lane, looked about in the same way and made a sign to their companions when they discovered nobody. Thereupon a rider appeared on a white horse who had a corpse behind him with the head and arms hanging down on one side and the legs on the other and supported on both sides by the two men who had first appeared. The procession advanced to the place where the refuse is thrown into the river. At the bank they came to a halt and turned the horse with its tail to the river. Then they lifted the corpse, one holding it by its hands and arms, the other by the legs and feet, dragged it down from the horse and cast it with all their strength into the river.

To the question of the rider if it was safely in, they answered, "Yes, Sir!" Then the rider cast another look at the river and, seeing the cloak of the corpse floating on the water, asked his companions what that black thing was floating there. They answered, "the cloak," whereupon he threw stones at the garment to make it sink to the bottom. Then all five, including the other two who had kept watch and now rejoined the rider and his two companions, departed and took their way together through another lane that leads to the Hospital of Saint James.

The servants of the Pope asked Giorgio why he had lodged no information of such a crime with the governor of the city, to which he answered: "In my day I have seen as many as a hundred corpses thrown into the river at that place on different nights without anybody troubling himself about it, and so I attached no further importance to the circumstance."

After this fishermen and boatmen were summoned from all Rome and ordered to drag the corpse out of the river with the assurance of a large reward for their pains.

Three hundred fishmen and boatmen, as I have heard, came together and dragged the bed of the river, and finally brought up the corpse of a man.

It was just before vespers when they found the duke still fully clad, with his stockings, shoes, coat, waistcoat and cloak, and in his belt there was his purse with thirty ducats. He had nine wounds, one in the neck through the throat, the other eight in the head, body and legs. The duke was laid in a boat and was carried into the castle of San Angelo, where his clothing was removed. The corpse was then washed and clothed in princely raiment. Everything was done at the order of my colleague, Bernardino Gutieri, cleric in charge of ceremonies.

On the evening of this day, at nine o'clock the corpse of the duke was brought by his noble retainers, if I remember rightly, from the castle of San Angelo to the church of Santa Maria del Popolo, preceded by 120 torchbearers and all the prelates of the palace, together with the papal servitors and pages. With loud lamentations and weeping they proceeded without any orderly formation. The corpse was borne upon a bier with pomp and ceremony in public view and looked more as if sleeping than dead. In the aforementioned church it was consigned to the vault, where it reposes up to the present day.

When the Pope was informed that the duke had been murdered and thrown into the river like refuse and there discovered, violent grief overcame him, and in his deep sorrow he locked himself in his chambers and wept bitterly. Only after long pleading, persuasion and solicitation before his door did the Cardinal Bartolommeo Marti finally succeed after several hours in being admitted with a few attendants. The Pope took no food or drink from the evening of Wednesday, the 14th of June, until the following Saturday, and he let no sleep come to his eyes from the morning of Thursday until the next Sunday. Upon varied and ceaseless appeals of his trusted friends he admitted himself to be won over and finally began to conquer his grief as well as he could. This he did also out of consideration for the risk and danger to his own person.

# IX

## LIFE IN ROME UNDER THE BORGIAS

ON the evening of the 28th of October, 1497, the secretary of the Pope, Bartolommeo Florido, formerly Archbishop of Cosenza, who had recently been deprived of all his honors, dignities, rank and livings in the Castle of San Angelo, was forced to lay off all his vestments. A cowl of coarse white cloth which hung down half a span below the knee was put on over his shirt instead of his tunic. He received a pair of shoes of the roughest leather, a coat of green cloth which almost reached the ground and was also very coarse and thick, and a coarse white cap. In his hands he was given a rather large wooden crucifix. In this attire he was brought from the chamber in which he had until then been held prisoner to the burial vault of the Emperor Hadrian called San Marocco, which had been designated as his life-long prison.

There stood for him a common wooden bed with a canopy to protect his head from the moisture of the stone walls. Upon the bed lay a straw pallet and a mattress with two coarse blankets. He was given a breviary, a Bible, and the letters of Saint Peter. Furthermore he received a keg of water, three loaves of bread, a cup of oil and a lamp for lighting. There he was incarcerated for the term of his life.

The Pope, as I was told, has given the order that the warden of the castle or his deputy should visit the prisoner every day or every three days and that bread and water should be portioned out to him for his maintenance and oil for his light. May Almighty God in all his mercy and loving kindness bestow upon this most miserable man the gift of patience and grant him grace that he may save his soul.

The report was that before this the Pope had daily dispatched to the imprisoned Florido in the castle of San Angelo the suffragan bishop of Toul, John Marades, the archdeacon de Bacchis, Petrus de Solis, and a few others of his trusted servants to play dice and chess with him and to lead him through proper persuasion to the confession that he had drawn up various *breves* without the order of the Pope. For the Pope thought thus to obtain forgiveness for other *breves* that had been drawn upon his order and had offended the King and Queen of Spain on the plea that they had been issued without his foreknowledge. If Florido would admit this, the Pope would raise his rank and reward him with higher offices. At their repeated instigation he had confessed, and thereafter neither Marades nor the others had ever visited him again.

On Sunday, the 29th of October, at 11 o'clock in the morning, the main tower of the castle of San Angelo was struck by lightning where the powder for the defense of the castle was stored. The explosion scattered far and wide the whole upper part of the tower together with the walls and the great marble angel, part of which fell near the house of Cardinal Michaeli beside the church of Saint Celsus and the near the house of the merchants Spannocchi. About fifteen guards of the castle were injured, but none of them mortally.

On Wednesday, the 14th of February, 1498, there was found in the river the papal groom of the chamber, Petrus Caldes, with the surname Peritto, who had fallen involuntarily into the Tiber on Thursday last, the 8th of February, during the night, an event which aroused much comment in Rome.

On Wednesday, the 21st of February, the cardinals and Cesare Borgia rode for their pleasure in French layman's garments from Rome to Ostia on the mouth of the Tiber, and returned to Rome in the same garments on the 24th.

At the carnival of this year no feast or public amusement was held in Rome or in Agone or in Testaccio, nor did any masked procession take place.

Last Sunday, the 18th, Giulio Vitelli of Corneto, a servant of Cardinal Domenico delle Rovere, was just attending mass in the convent church of the Dominicans sopra Minerva, when some one entered the church with about ten companions in arms carrying concealed crossbows and bearing long and short swords, lances and round shields. They rushed into the Chapel of Crucifixion, toward Giulio and his brothers and wounded them, and of these wounds Giulio and two of his brothers died within a few days.

After breakfast time on Sunday the governor rode with a large suite to the house of the aforesaid.

On Ash Wednesday, the 28th of February, 1498, the Pope pronounced the benediction over the ashes in the main chapel of the palace. First the officiating Cardinal Groslaye strewed ashes upon him, then he on the cardinal, and then on the others in the accustomed manner. Guglielmo Serra of the order of the Minorites in surplice and pluviale without a mitre, preached the sermon, and kissed the foot of the Pope because he was not yet an ordained bishop. The rest of the ceremony proceeded in the usual manner.

Cardinal Cesare Borgia did not attend the mass and service. After the mass in response to my request the Pope granted to us, the masters of ceremony, to all the singers and to the other members of the papal chapel the permission for every one of us to choose a confessor to absolve us from all sins, even from those which could be forgiven by the Holy See alone.

Through daily worship at the main altar of Saint Peter's we were also to obtain the indulgence of the stations in the city.  While the Pope was laying off the sacred vestments in the Camera Papagalli, he ordered the Datarious Giovanni Ferrari, Bishop of Modena, that he should inscribe me on the preferential list of his confidential men of long standing and give me equal rank with my colleague, Bernardino Gutteri.

A few days before, at the beginning of April, 1498, a courtesan, that is, an honest prostitute, named Cursetta, had been thrown into prison because she had a Moor as a friend who went around in women's clothing under the name of the Spanish Barbara, and had relations with her.  Both of them, therefore, as a punishment for this outrage, were led around together through the city, she clad in a loose black velvet dress open from neck to ankle, the Moor in a woman's dress which was taken up to the shirt, that is to the navel, in order that everybody might see his private parts and recognize the fraud he had perpetrated.  During this his arms were tightly bound together above the elbows behind his back.

After the procession in public Cursetta was let go, but the Moor was put in prison and finally led out on Saturday, the 7th of April, from the prison of

Torre di Nona together with two other brigands with a *Sbirre* riding before them on an ass carrying on the point of a stick two testicles, which had been cut out from a Jew because he had had intercourse with a Christian woman. They were brought to the Flora field where the two brigands were hanged. The Moor was placed on a pile of wood, and was killed on the pole of the gallows, a rope being tied about his neck whereby he was strung fast to the pole. Then the pile was lighted, but on account of a downpour of rain it did not burn well and only his legs were charred.

On the 21st of April, 1498, in the evening or during the night the major-domo of the Apostolic palace, the Bishop of Calahorra, Petrus de Aranda, was locked up in his chamber in the palace and a guard was placed before his door until the 26th of April, on which day he was conducted before the Pope. After a conversation with him he was brought into the chambers between the two secret gardens of the Pope, not far from the covered walk that leads from the palace to the castle of San Angelo. There he was guarded carefully by the grooms of the Pope and others until about the middle of September. The reason for his imprisonment was that the bishop was being suspected of heresy, being a marano, and similar offenses.

On Sunday, the 29th of July, 1498, a large and spacious platform was erected before two porticos

of St. Peter's Church.    There a hundred-and-eighty
*maranoes* [1] were admitted in order to be reconciled
to the faith.    There they were cowering down on
the floor in their everyday garments and there sat
also the Archbishop of Reggio and Governor of
Rome, Pietro Isuagli, the ambassador of the King
and Queen of Spain, Juan Ruiz de Medina, the
Bishop Octavius de Monte Marano, referendary of
the Pope, the auditors Dominicus Jacobatius and
Jacobus Dragnatius, the professors of theology, Paul
de Modia of the order of the Predicants, and Johannes de Malcone of the order of the Minorites,
both papal penitentiaries in St. Peter's church for
the Spanish nation, also in their everyday garments.
A master of theology of the order of the Predicants
preached a sermon on the faith in Italian and reproached the *maranoes*, who were all Spaniards,
among them a Franciscan monk, for their errors
in faith, reprimanding and instructing them.    After
the sermon the *maranoes* asked for a remission of sins
and absolution.    Thereupon Paul de Mondia admonished them in a Latin address to adhere to the right
faith and to lead a righteous life, and told them of
the punishment they all deserved.    This admonition
he explained to them in a few words in Spanish.
Then while they were all down on their knees, he

---

[1] Maranoes were called those Jews and Moors who, during
the persecution by the Spanish Inquisition, professed to be
Catholics while secretly adhering to their own religion.

pronounced the punishment upon them, namely, that they should walk two and two to the church of St. Peter in a garment prescribed and worn for this purpose. There they should pray and then go in the same order to the church of the convent of Santa Maria sopra Minerva, where every one of them might lay down the garment and return to his home. The magisters Paul and John announced the absolution to all, whereupon they started on their way to the church. The Pope observed all that was going on from the new chambers and gave them the benediction.

The garment in which the *maranoes* were clad looked as follows: over their every day clothes they wore coverings of red and peacock-blue cloth which were hung down over the shoulders up on the breast and down to the legs behind, with a yellow cross four fingers in width and of the length of the cloth. Before the altar in Santa Maria sopra Minerva every one put down his cloth. The monks then hung up the cloth in the church in memory of the event.

In this year, 1499, all the feasts of the Roman carnival were celebrated. On Sunday in Lent, the 3rd of February, the Jews held their race from the Campo dei Fiori to the castle San Angelo near the Borgo-Gate for the price of a red cloth, which, however, was not handed over on that day as the start was bad, as has been reported.

Therefore they ran another time on Monday, the 4th of February, after vespers from the Campo dei Fiori, that is to say from the corner between the houses of the Vice-chancellor and the Lord Coronato de Planca, as far as the place of St. Peter.

On Tuesday, the 5th of February, the young men ran after dinner for a rose-colored cloth from the aforementioned corner to the place of St. Peter.

On Wednesday, the 6th, the old men ran for a red cloth from the chapels to the place.

On Thursday, the 7th, there was a fête on the Agone which was well prepared according to Roman custom. Even the papal privy Chamberlain, John Marades, had masked himself and sat on the back of a horse which knocked slightly against some Romans, whereupon he came into danger of being wounded, unknown as he was, had not those who stood around intervened. It was prohibited, therefore, on the following day to mask oneself, but this was not observed by any one.

On the same Thursday or Friday there was also a Spanish priest killed by masked men. The same priest had killed the brother of one of the masks in Spain. This priest resembled me in his clothes perhaps or in some other way. Several cardinals, Carafa, San Giorgio, Caravajal, Piccolomini and Farnese made inquiries whether the rumor was true, as did also many other curials. The rumor about me circulated for three days.  May Almighty God in His eternal kindness preserve me from such and all other dangers!

On Friday, the 8th of February, 1499, the bulls were caught and distributed over the various districts of the city, and on Saturday evening they were brought in the usual way to the Capitol.

On Sunday, the 10th of February, there was held a race of the Berber steeds, the Spanish saddle horses and the mares after dinner in Testaccio for the usual prizes.  The first and third Cardinal Sanseverino received, and he would also have won the second had not a rider fallen down.  The second prize was received by John Franciscus Mutus.  Then the feast of the bulls and pigs was celebrated in the customary way and without uproar and scandal.

On Monday, the 11th, after dinner the race of the donkeys was held, with a sky blue cloth as a prize, from the Campo dei Fiori to the Place of St. Peter, and Shrove Tuesday, the 12th, in the same way the race of the buffaloes for a red cloth.

# X

## THE AGGRANDIZEMENT OF THE BORGIAS

YESTERDAY, the 16th of February, 1499, Donna Lucretia, the daughter of the Pope, went for walk in the arbor, fell down in a faint and as a result had a miscarriage of a female child with which she was pregnant.

On Saturday, the 20th of April, 1499, the Pope received a letter from France advising him that the marriage contract had been concluded by the former Cardinal Cesare Borgia and the Lord d'Albret in the name of his daughter, by which, as was reported, and as it was in fact set down in the contract, the Pope was to give a dowry of 200,000 ducats, and the marriage was not to be performed until his Holiness had nominated the brother of the bride a cardinal.

On the 23rd of May, 1499, a courier arrived from France with the report for the Pope that his son Cesare, the former cardinal, had contracted the marriage with the Lady d'Albret, on Sunday, the 12th of May, and had performed it and did take her eight times, one after the other. Another messenger announced, the King of France had received the duke on Pentecost, the 19th of May, into the Fraternity of St. Michael which is royal and very glorious. Therefore by the order of the Pope numerous fires were lighted in the city on the evening of the 23rd of May, namely before the houses of the Cardinals Orsini and Groslaye, of Lucretia and many Spaniards, as a sign of joy, but a great shame and scandal for the Pope and the Holy See.

On Saturday, the 20th of July, at eight o'clock in the evening, the Pope received a report, that the major-domo of Cesare Borgia, Jacobus, who on Friday, the 12th of July, had walked apparently quite unconcerned through the halls of the palace while the secret consistory was being held, and who had secretly mounted his horse after the consistory was over in order to betake himself as fast as possible through the gates in the name of the Pope with secret messages for his master, had been seized and searched by the Duke of Milan and all his secret despatches surrendered. The Pope, frightened at the news, had the gates of the city closed and guarded, and no one was let out without the permission of the governor. The servants of the Vice-chancellor Ascanio Sforza, and the ambassador of the Duke of Milan had been informed of this, however, through a letter of the duke that had arrived in the morning. Therefore all his servants and the prelates fled from the house of the Vice-chancellor.

Their belongings they brought out already in the morning. The Archbishop of Sutri, Alatri, the Prothonotaries Marini and Sforza took refuge in the house of Cardinal Colonna. A certain Bartholomeus, the chamberlain of the Vice-chancellor, was seized and brought into the castle of San Angelo, but he was not hurt and was soon set at liberty again. The Pope in his excitement sent the Governor of Rome to Cardinal Colonna and with him his secretary, the Prothonotary Adriano, with the request that the cardinal should send the prelates, the Prothonotaries Marini and Sforza, to his Holiness, a request which the cardinal, however, politely refused. Thereupon ensued an exchange of views for many hours between the cardinal and the governor, the answer of the cardinal being reported to the Pope and that of the latter to the cardinal. Finally, when he saw that there was perhaps danger threatening, he left the house secretly with the prelates and the others, who had fled to him, while the governor and Adriano were in his room, and departed from the city for his castle at two o'clock in the night.

When the governor and Adriano had waited for some time for the decision of the cardinal, they realized that they had been deceived and returned to the Pope, who became excited and at about or after midnight summoned the chief of the Apostolic Chancery and the deputy of the Vice-chancellor, Bishop Aloysius of Pesaro, and upon his arrival had him placed under detention in the room of the Datary Ferrari, Bishop of Modena, and guarded by the datary himself. Finally on Sunday after dinner he set him free and sent him back to his house. On the same Sunday in the morning the governor went by order of the Pope with all his men to the house of the Vice-chancellor and searched it. After about two hours he went away again without having disturbed anything there.

On the same Saturday evening before seven o'clock the Bishop of Aquina, Baptista Buffallus, was returning home on horseback from the house of the Cardinal Orsini, when one of his enemies assaulted him not far from Monte Giorgdano and wounded him with his sword. It was rumored, thereupon, that the bishop had been killed. He finally arrived, however, only slightly hurt, at his own house.

On Tuesday, the 23rd of July, 1499, the Vice-chancellor, Cardinal Ascanio, boarded at the Colonnese Neptuno Castro a ship of King Federigo of Naples, which was lying ready for him there and under the escort of three other royal ships set his course for Piombino in order to go to Milan. He then left the ship in the territory of Siena and wrote from there to the Pope and the Holy colleague asking for leave and stating the reasons of his departure.

On Friday, the 2nd of August, 1499, before daybreak, Alphonso of Aragon, Duke of Bisceglia, the husband of Lucretia Borgia, departed secretly from Rome in order to reach the Colonnese territory. From there he went to the King of Naples, and this without the permission, knowledge or consent of the Pope.

On Thursday, the 8th of August, 1499, Lucretia Borgia departed from the city through the Porta del Popolo, to go to the Castle of Spoleto, of which she had been appointed governor by the Pope. She was accompanied by Don Gofredo Borgia of Aragon, her brother, who rode at her left, and sent many laden sumpters in advance which the Pope inspected from the loggia. When she and her brother had mounted their horses or mules in the place of St. Peter at the foot of the steps of the church, they made a very reverential obeisance from their horses to the Pope, who stood above, and took their last leave of him. After the Pope had blessed them from the window for the third time they rode away. Before them there marched in good order the whole palace guard of the Pope and the governor of Rome with his men. In the train was also a mule which had been laden with a stretcher and mattress, a crimson cover strewn with flowers, two pillows of white damask and a beautiful canopy so that Donna Lucretia could rest there in case she was tired from riding. Another mule bore a saddle upon which was erected a silk covered and magnificently adorned arm-chair with back and footstool, in order that Donna Lucretia might sit in it from time to time and travel more comfortably. From the place of St. Peter as far as the bridge of San Angelo she was escorted on her right by the ambassador of the King of Naples and later by the governor of Rome, while there followed after, two by two, the prelates and a large crowd in honor and praise of the Holy See.

On the 1st of November, 1499, at six o'clock in the morning, Donna Lucretia was delivered of a boy. This was announced by order of the Pope to all the cardinals and ambassadors and to his other friends even before daybreak in their residences. The messengers received for this from every cardinal and ambassador two ducats, more or less, according to the mood of the giver.

On the feast of St. Martin, Monday, the 11th of November, the son of Lucretia, Rodrigo, was christened by Cardinal Carafa in the chapel of Pope Sixtus IV in St. Peter's. On the day before the chapel of the Cardinal Zeno in St. Peter's had been put in readiness for the event and adorned with two large rugs which covered the wall at the right and left as well as the bench and floor before the bench. The altar had no decoration, only a plain and rather soiled and tattered cover. In this chapel gathered all the cardinals present in Rome, sixteen in number.

The house of Cardinal Zeno, where the lady in childbed resided, was also adorned magnificently: the two portals were completely gilded, the whole courtyard, the lower staircase and the first hall were covered with cloth and carpets, the first chamber with sky-blue velvet, the bed with crimson. Everywhere there were carpets on the floor and benches were standing around. In this house there gathered the prelates of the palace and the ambassadors. In the meantime about sixty Roman ladies called on the lady in childbed. Those who were present at the christening included the Imperial Ambassador Philibertus Naturelli, the ambassador of the King of England, Silvester, the ambassadors of Naples, Venice, Savoy, Florence and Siena.

When all the cardinals had assembled they proceeded from the chapel, where they had met, to the Sixtine chapel, the tribune of which was adorned with cloth of gold brocade. The monument of Sixtus was covered with the same cloth and there were large carpets everywhere. The child to be christened, as it had not yet been prepared, was brought from the house of St. Peter's up to the railing of the Sixtine chapel by special permission and dispensation of the Pope and in the following order: there marched first the papal shield-bearers and behind them all the chamberlains in pink garments as on Corpus-Christi day. Then there came drummers with pipes and other instruments. There followed two papal shield-bearers of whom the one at the right carried a golden basin with a goblet and in the basin was a golden salt cellar with salt and a box with musk soap and a towel; the other one at the left carried a large candle of white wax, weighing about thirteen pounds adorned with gold and very magnificent workmanship. These were followed by Juan Cervillon of Catalonia, formerly captain of the papal soldiers, who carried the child on his right arm. It was covered with brocade lined with ermine as one usually covers children to be christened. At the right walked the governor of Rome and at the left the Imperial Ambassador Philibertus all two by two, and a numerous crowd closed the procession. At the entrance of the Sixtine chapel Juan Cervillon handed over the child to the Archbishop of Cosenza, Francesco Borgia, who took him on his right arm that is in the silken cloth magnificently interwoven with gold which Juan had carried slung around his neck. Cardinal Juan Carafa came to the entrance of the chapel and catechized the child and then had it brought into the chapel to the space between the altar and the monument of Sixtus IV. There in the center on a stool covered with a rug stood the large Sixtine baptismal vessel of silver, partly gilded. On this spot the afore-mentioned silk cloth was put around the shoulders of the governor of Rome, who thereupon took the child to be christened upon his right arm from the hands of the Archbishop of Cosenza. The cardinal moistened the head of the child and baptized it and did everything in the usual way while the secretary Podocatoro and the Datary

Ferrari held their hands over the child as god-fathers.

After the child had been baptized and the Cardinal Carafa and the godfathers had washed their hands as usual, Paolo Orsini put the silk cloth around his neck and took over the child from the governor upon his right arm and returned with it to the house of Cardinal Zeno. Even before he 'had come to the entrance of the chapel the child began to cry miserably, while before this, from its mother's bed to the chapel and throughout the baptismal ceremonies it had patiently submitted to everything without showing displeasure. On the returning from the church, however, there was such a noise from trumpets and other instruments that one could not even hear the sound of his own voice.

They returned in the same order as they had come. After them the cardinals also left the church, mounted their mules at the foot of the stairs of the church and returned home. On the way to the christening a crowd of Roman women, old men, young men and maidens gathered and followed behind the prelates who sat down here and there in the Sixtine chapel on the seats higher up.

On Monday, the 18th of November, 1499, Cesare Borgia returned secretly through the Porta Cavallegieri to Rome with a chamberlain and the brother of the deceased John Marades and stayed with the Pope in the palace until Thursday, the 21st. On

the morning of this day he departed and rode away
secretly with an escort of papal soldiers to the city of
Imola, which he took over soon afterward by force
together with the castle.   The Lords of the city, the
sons of the deceased Count Girolamo Riario, nephew
of Cardinal Riario, were robbed with violence.

On the same Thursday after dinner the Cardinal
Riario rode out with his household to hunt.   When
he was near the " castrum Jubilei " he sent his chamberlain Cardilla back to Rome with the greater number of his suite, while he himself rode on with a few
attendants to Monte Rotondo.

In the evening of the same day a papal musician,
Thomasius of Forli, was arrested with his accomplices and incarcerated in the castle of San Angelo.
This Thomasius had come to Rome with a poisoned
letter which he put into a reed to give it to the Pope,
pretending that he came from the community of
Forli which wanted an agreement with the Pope.
Had the Pope accepted the letter, he would have been
poisoned and would have fallen down dead within a
few days or hours.   In order to obtain access to
the Pope, he approached a friend, Thomasius of
Forli, a musician of Juan Borgia, the prince of
Squillace, and then bribed a guard of the portal
of the papal palace, whom he initiated into his under-
taking.   This came to the knowledge of the Pope
and they were imprisoned by his orders as has been
told.   When questioned they immediately admitted

everything.    The leader was especially questioned as to whether he had thought that he could ever get away with his life after having perpetrated such a misdeed.    He answered that he had had the firm hope that through the death of the Pope, Imola and Forli might be freed from the blockade of Cesare and that peace and tranquillity might thus be restored to the ruler of these cities, the widow of Count Girolamo, his patroness, who had aided him from his youth. If he could die for her ten times, he would be ready to suffer death and would not be afraid.

On Friday, the 29th of November, 1499, Donna Lucretia left the house for the first time after the birth of the child and visited the church of St. Peter's.    The Bishop of Carignola, Petrus Gamboa, conducted her by the left arm to and from the church and celebrated the mass for her.    I have also heard that Donna Lucretia spent the previous evening in the company of her father, the Pope.

During the night from Sunday to Monday, the 23rd of December, 1499, the noble knight, Juan Cervillon of Catalona, formerly captain of the papal soldiers, who lived with many in hostile relations, had ordered a meal in the house of the nobleman Elisaeus de Pignatello of Naples, a knight of the order of St. John.    The house stood opposite the residence of Cardinal Ascania Sforza, in an alley through which one came straight to the place past Ascanio's stable.    Cervillon had spent the evening before the meal in 'the house of Cardinal Carvajal, who knew much about his feuds and admonished him in a fatherly way that he should not leave more his house this evening. Also he ordered his servants they should not let out Cervillon. Nevertheless, as Pignatello, who was waiting for him, had sent for him several times up to twelve o'clock, he left the house of Cardinal Carvajal at about that hour, and repaired to the house of Pignatello, where he ate. In addition to these two, Cervillon and Pignatello, there partook of the meal a nephew of Cervillon, one of their friends, and a lady of the papal court. After the meal Cervillon was for leaving the house again but Pignatello objected with all his might. When he found that all his arts of persuasion were of no avail he besought him that at least his nephew, who was armed, and a few of his servants should escort him, but Cervillon firmly declined and said that he desired no escort. They urged him to permit at least that some one should go out before him to look around and see if there was any suspicious person passing or lying in wait. Even this he would not permit but he wanted to go out free and unaccompanied. So he fared forth from the house about one o'clock in the night, armed only with his sword and paused not far from the entrance. As he stood there, two men approached him and asked: " Who goes there? " He answered " Good friend! " When they asked in a more pressing manner: " What good friend? " he added, " Juan Cervillon." As soon as he had said this they jumped at him and one sword while the other severed his head with one blow, and both escaped.

When the nephew and the others within the house heard the voice of Cervillon and the clash of swords, they ran out to see what had happened. They found Juan Cervillon lying on the wall and his head a short distance off on the ground but no trace of those who had committed the deed. On the following morning the incident was reported to the Pope by the governor of Rome, who on the very night of the murder of Cervillon had displayed the greatest energy upon receiving the news and had questioned Pignatello as well as all the other inhabitants of the house with the greatest care about everything that had happened. This he reported to the Pope in my presence and added that when the nephew and the others had rushed out and had found Cervillon dead and no one in the street, they had hurried farther along the street and had presently met a boy of whom they inquired if he had seen anybody. He answered, no, only two men, who had walked through the alley and had fled over the large open place before the stable of the Vice-chancellor. Thus ended poor Cervillon with a bitter death. His body was soon afterward brought by his servants to the church of Santa Maria Transpontina and there buried without pomp.

# XI

# THE YEAR OF THE JUBILEE

FEBRUARY, 1500. In former days the major-domo of the papal palace, Petrus de Aranda, Bishop of Calahorra, had been arrested as suspected of heresy, and brought to the castle San Angelo, where he was imprisoned. The governor of Rome, Cardinal Isuagli, and the Bishop of Cesena, Pietro Menzi, as deputy-auditors of the papal camera, had been charged with the investigation and procedure. To justify himself Aranda brought up, as I was later informed, a hundred witnesses who, however, all without exception gave evidence against him. It was ascertained that he asserted and maintained among other things that the Mosaic law had only one principle, while the Christian had three, Father, Son and Holy Ghost, that Christ had not suffered as a real God, and that he had in praying said " Gloria Patri " leaving away " Filio " and " Spiritu sancto," that he had eaten before celebrating the mass and had eaten meat on Good Friday and other forbidden days, that he had stated that indulgences were void and inefficacious and had been invented by the fathers

119

for their own advantage, and that there was no hell
or purgatory but only paradise, and many other
things.

On the 25th of February, 1500, a papal letter
was posted at the doors of St. Peter's and the Lateran Church which stated that the roads and inns for
the pilgrims to Rome ought to be safeguarded during the year of the jubilee and that the vassals of the
Church would be held responsible for damage sus-
tained and that reprisals would be made against
them.

On Monday, the 26th of February, 1500, by order
of the Pope it was urged upon all the cardinals that
they should send their suites on this day at four
o'clock in the afternoon out to the Porta Santa
Maria del Popolo to meet Cesare Borgia as he approached the city and furthermore upon all ambassadors, conservators and officials of Rome as well as
upon the abbreviators, clerics, etc., of the Roman
Curia that they should go out personally to meet him.
On the previous Friday, the 21st, Cardinal Orsini
had gone to meet the Duke Cesare as far as Castello;
and there followed him on Saturday, the 22nd, the
Cardinal Farnese.  On this morning the Cardinal
Lopez, with my colleague in his suite, went out to
meet him about three to four miles beyond the Ponte
Molle.  All the ambassadors also rode out beyond
the bridge as far as the meadows to await the duke
there.  When it had sounded the hour of four Car-

dinal Pallavicini went on horseback from the palace to the residence of Cardinal Orsini who awaited him there outside on his mule. They rode together to the church of Santa Maria del Popolo to receive the duke there. He entered through the gate between seven and eight o'clock and was greeted by all the ambassadors, retainers and officials of the said cardinal. When they heard that the duke was outside the gate, they mounted their mules and awaited him at the said place before the gate, where they saluted him with bared heads while he thanked them also in the same manner. Then he rode between them to the Vatican.

In the train of the duke there came first in good order a hundred sumpters provided with new black covers and then about fifty others without any order. I could not arrange the escort in proper order as there were about a thousand ducal soldiers on foot, Swiss and Gascons, who marched in their own order in five sections and under five banners with the ducal arms, and took no heed of our order. There were also papal soldiers marching on foot to meet the duke and lansquenets with the flag of St. Andrew. The Swiss wanted the lansquenets to roll up their banner but they would not consent and a great quarrel started among them. But the conflict was settled by the duke with little effort. The Swiss and Gascons marched first with their banners, behind them came the lansquenets with theirs, and then about fifty noblemen of the duke. He himself had a hundred men around him of whom every one bore a new halberd and wore a coat of black velvet and shoes of black cloth.

He had also many trumpeters wearing his arms as well as two heralds of his own and one of the King of France, who wanted to march under all conditions behind the soldiers. The duke, however, when appealed to, decided that he ought to precede them, which he did only with great reluctance. By order of the duke the trumpeters and the other musicians did not play.

Behind them rode the Duke of Bisceglia at the right and the Prince of Squillace, the son of the Pope, at the left. Then came the duke between the aforementioned cardinals, behind them the Archbishop of Ragusa, de Sachis, at the right and the Bishop of Tréguier, Robert Guibé, Ambassador of the King of France, at the left, the Bishop of Zamora at the right and the ambassador of the King of Spain at the left, and so on, the others according to their rank. Two ambassadors of the King of Navarre got into a quarrel with the ambassadors of the Kings of Naples and of England, who retorted in a very hotheaded manner. The two ambassadors of Navarre had to give in and departed. There were also present the ambassadors of Florence, Venice, Savoy, and others. Behind them followed a large crowd in such confusion that the prelates were not able to take their places and the majority of them therefore departed.

The Pope stood in the loggia of the chamber above the portal of the palace, and with him were the Cardinals Juan Borgia, San Giorgio, Lopez, Cesarini and Farnese. When the duke came to the chamber of paraments, the Pope entered the Camera Papagalli, bringing with him five cushions of gold brocade, one of which he had laid on the elevated seat where he himself sat, another one under his feet and the three others upon the floor before his footstool. The door to the Camera Papagalli was opened and there entered the noblemen of the duke and after them, between the cardinals, the duke himself, who knelt down before the Pope and made a short speech in Spanish wherein he thanked the Pope that he had deigned to do him during his absence such a — I do not know what. The Pope replied to him in the same idiom, which I did not understand. Then the duke kissed both feet of the Pope as well as his right hand and was allowed also to kiss his mouth. After the duke the noblemen also approached at their pleasure to kiss the foot.

The castle of San Angelo was splendidly decorated and I never saw such pomp and triumph as from this castle.

On Thursday, the 27th of February, 1500, there was a festive procession in the Agone with the customary gorgeous display, twelve triumphal chariots and the victory of Julius Cæsar, who sat on the last chariot. All these chariots were taken to the palace and back again with the exception of the last one with Julius Cæsar, which remained there. The duke rode from the palace to the Agone where the festivities of the Romans were held in the customary way.

On Thursday, the 5th of March, Cesare Borgia began with his calls on the cardinals. He had no bishop or prelate with him but was only accompanied by one of his retainers. When calling on Cardinal Piccolomini he went with him from the chamber down to the foot of the stairs walking on his left side, as he did not want to take the right one in any case, although the cardinal offered it to him with eager insistency. As I hear, he did the same with the other cardinals but I do not know how far the cardinals went to meet him when he arrived and therefore I could not put it down.

On the fourth Sunday of Lent the Pope, with the intention of making Cesare Borgia Captain-General and Gonfaloniere of the Roman Church, decided to bestow upon him the Golden Rose.[1] On Sunday Laetare, therefore, the fourth of Lent and the 29th of March, 1500, the Pope had come into the small audience room in the morning at the usual hour with the cardinals, who had assembled in the Camera Papagalli, and decided with their consent to bestow the aforesaid Rose on Cesare Borgia of France, Duke of Valentinois, his dearest son, and to nominate him

[1] See page 19.

Captain-General and Gonfaloniere of the Holy Roman
Church. From there the Pope went with the cardinals into the chamber, blessed the Rose in the customary way, and went in procession on his portable
chair with the Rose in his left hand to the church of
St. Peter. Immediately before him walked a papal
shield-bearer in a garment of frilled brocade which
came down to his knees. He walked before the chamberlains and carried over his arm a new garment,
that is a coat and barret, the insignia of the dignity
of a Gonfaloniere. The barret was of crimson, two
spans high, and lined with ermine. In the middle
there was a small piece of gold brocade with four
large buttons, that is to say pearls of the size of
ordinary nuts. At the four corners and inside there
was a stripe of ermine fur about five fingers broad
and above there was attached a dove composed of
pearls, four fingers wide and adorned with many
pearls. While the Pope was still sitting in his portable chair, Cardinal Cibó appeared, who was officiating in the church, and dressed himself as usual
in the sandals and the holy garments. After arriving at the main altar the Pope took down the mitre
and prayed in his folding-chair; then he made the
confession of faith together with the celebrant.

In the meantime the duke stepped up to the papal
throne and placed himself at the right side. After
the obeisance of the cardinals the duke in his short
tunic stepped before the Pope and kneeled down

before him at the last step above. He was joined
by the Cardinal delle Rovere as an assistant of the
Pope, who now with the mitre in his hand rose and
said: "Our assistance in the name of the Lord who
made heaven and earth. The Lord be with you and
with your spirit.—Let us pray: 'God, who Thou
has promised to be an aid to Thy servants assembled
in Thy name, grant to this Thy servant Cesare, our
Gonfaloniere, the mercy that has been granted to
Abraham at the burnt offering, to Moses with his
legions, to Elia in the desert, to Samuel in the temple. Give, O Lord, the unity, that Thou gavest to
the patriarchs, that Thou hast preached to the
peoples, that Thou hast handed down to the
Apostles, that Thou hast ordered to the victors.
Bless, O Lord, we ask Thee, this our Gonfaloniere,
who has been given to us certainly for the welfare of
our people. Let him grow rich in years, let him be
blooming and healthy in vigor of body until a ripe
old age and let him arrive finally at a blessed end.
May the trust remain with us that he will receive
the same compassion in favor of his people that
Aaron received in the sanctuary, Elisha by the
stream, Ezekiel on his bed and the old Zachary in
the temple. May the force and power of dominion
be granted to him as Joshua possessed it in the
camp and Gideon in battle, and as Peter received it
with the keys and Paul used it in doctrine. Thus the

care of the shepherds may be a blessing to the sheep as Isaac prospered in his fruits and Jacob in his herds. This grant us mercifully the One who lives and reigns with the Father and the Holy Ghost in eternity.' "

After these words the Pope put the mitre on his head and sat down again. I took the coat from the hands of that shield-bearer, and handed it over to the assisting Cardinal delle Rovere who took off the coat of the duke. I received it and had it sent quickly through my servant to my house before anything further was said about it. For it was worth about four hundred ducats. The Pope took the coat from the hands of Cardinal delle Rovere and hung it around the duke, so that the clasp was lying on the right shoulder of the duke, with the following words: " May the Lord clothe you with this garment of blessing and wrap you in the garb of joy, in the name of the Father, the Son and the Holy Ghost. Amen."

Then the same cardinal took from my hands the aforementioned crimson barret and handed it over to the Pope, who put it on the head of the duke with these words: " Receive the sign of the dignity of the Gonfaloniere that is being put on your head by us in the name of the Father, the Son and the Holy Ghost, and remember that from now on you are pledged to defend the faith and the Holy Church.

That success may be true to you, may be granted to you mercifully by Him that is blessed in all eternity."

A cleric of the Camera brought the Rose from the altar, and the Pope took it from the hands of the Cardinal delle Rovere and handed it over to the duke who knelt before him with the following words: " Receive from our hands as we are, although undeservedly God's representative on earth, as a symbol of the joy of Jerusalem triumphant as well as of the church militant. To all who believe in Christ it means the most precious flower as it is the joy and crown of all saints. Receive it, my most-beloved son, you who are of secular nobility, powerful and rich in virtue, in order that you may win furthermore the nobility of every virtue in Christ, the Lord, similar to the Rose that has been planted on the bank of many waters. This favor may grant you in its overflowing kindness the One who is the triune in eternity. Amen."

The duke took the Rose in his right hand and kissed first the hand then the foot of the Pope. Both rose, the duke covered himself with the barret, and with the Rose in his right hand, walked, for the entire time, before the Pope. The holy handkerchief was shown as usual and the cardinals besides the duke accompanied the Pope as far as the courtyard, where the cardinals usually ride away. From there the Pope went up to his palace after he had dismissed the duke and the cardinals, who then all mounted their horses. The older cardinals rode first and last between Piccolomini and Cesarini, the duke still wearing the barret of the Gonfaloniere on his head. The Rose, however, he did not bear in his hand all the way, but he had it carried most of the way by one of his servants, of whom he had only six or eight around himself while the others followed.

In riding back the usual order was observed, the banners were carried by those two armed men on horseback, both Spaniards of the lower class. They rode behind all the ambassadors, preceded by eight trumpeters and before these four drummers. After the trumpeters there came three heralds, after these the armed men, then all the cardinals and among the last of these the cardinal with all his servants. There followed the prelates and the men of the duke in a crowd as this could not be helped. In this order we rode to the residence of Cardinal Sclafenata, where the duke intended to have dinner. Before the entrance the duke thanked with bared head every one of the cardinals, who had stopped here and there. Finally he turned around once again before the door to the cardinals who then departed.

On Tuesday, the 12th of May, 1500, a certain Baron René d'Agrimont, ambassador of the King of France, while on his way to Rome with his sumpters and about thirteen horses and servants was robbed completely by twenty-two highwaymen and brigands in the mountains of Viterbo. One of his noblemen together with a servant was wounded severely.

The ambassador entered Rome on the 13th May without pomp and escorted only by his men. The Pope, indignant at the incident, sent out the Bargello to capture the malefactors, and wrote numerous *breves* to Fabrizio Colonna, from whose territory the brigands had come, and to others in order that they should send the highwaymen to the city. Fifteen of them were apprehended and brought to Rome.

On Wednesday, 27th May, 1500, the day before Assumption, eighteen men were hanged at noon while the cardinals passed over the bridge of San Angelo, nine on each side of the bridge. The hanged men fell down with the gallows on the bridge but were immediately set up again so that the cardinals when they returned from the palace could see all of them hanged.

The first of the eighteen was a doctor of medicine, physician and surgeon to the hospital of St. John Lateran, who had left the hospital every day early in the morning in a short tunic and with a crossbow and had shot every one who happened to cross his path and pocketed his money. It was also said that the confessor of the hospital communicated with the physician when a patient confided to him during confession that he possessed any money, whereupon he gave an efficacious remedy to the patient and they divided the money between them. Thirteen belonged to the twenty-two who had robbed Baron d'Agrimont. The four others had committed various misdeeds.

After vespers, on the 28th of May, 1500, the eighteen hanged men were taken down, laid on carts, and brought to the chapel by the society of Misericordia, where they were buried in the usual way.

On Wednesday, the 24th of June, 1500, the feast of St. John, the place of St. Peter was railed in by beams on all sides from the corner of the house of the palace-guard to the fountain of Innocence and from there to the corner of the house St. Martinelli, as well as both approaches of the Via Sancta towards the church of St. Peter. After dinner a bullfight was held in this enclosure with five or six bulls. Cesare on horseback and several others administered numerous thrusts to them until they were dead.

On Wednesday, 15th July, 1500, the Duke Alphonse of Aragon, the husband of Lucretia Borgia, was suddenly attacked on the steps of St. Peter before the outer entrance about ten o'clock at night and severely wounded in the head, the right arm, and the leg. The assailants fled down the stairs of St. Peter, where about forty men on horseback were waiting for them and they rode out with these through the Porta Pertusa.

On Tuesday, 18th August, 1500, Alphonso of Aragon, who had been brought after his recent in-

juries to the new tower above the papal cellar in the
main garden of the Vatican, and had been carefully
guarded, was strangled in his bed at four o'clock in
the afternoon, as he did not die of his wounds. In
the evening at ten o'clock the body was carried to
the church of St. Peter and buried in the chapel of
Maria delle Febbri. The archbishop of Cosenza,
Francesco Borgia, the treasurer of the Pope, accompanied the body with their suites.

The physicians of the deceased and a hunchback
who had nursed him almost all the time were arrested and brought to the castle of San Angelo
where an investigation was started against them.
They were set free later on as they were found not
guilty, a fact that was very well known to those
who had made out the warrants.

The same day and almost at the same hour Lucas
de Dulcibus, the chamberlain of Cardinal delle Rovere and master of the Register of Papal Decrees,
was wounded to death on the back of his mule before
the house of the Roman citizen Domenico de Massimi, and his membrum virile was cut off by a man
of Reiti whose wife he had kept as a concubine. He
was brought into the house of the said Domenico
where he died after three or four hours. In the
evening he was carried to the church of Maria
Transpontina and the next morning, Wednesday, the
19th, the body was transferred to the church of
Santa Maria del Popolo with the suite of the Car-

dinal delle Rovere and many others in the funeral
procession.  May he rest in peace!

On Sunday, 23d August, 1500, there arrived in
Rome, Lord Lucas de Villeneuve, Baron de Trans,
chamberlain of the King of France and his ambassador.  To the inn of Domenico Attavanti, where
the ambassador stayed, near the hospital of St. Laz-
arus, a masked rider came in great haste, accompanied by a man on foot.  He dismounted, embraced
the ambassador with the mask over his face and had a
conversation with him.  After a short while the masked person returned to the city.  It has been said
that it was Cesare Borgia.

The ambassador mounted his horse and rode to
the city.  The suite of the Pope and of all the cardinals present in Rome went to meet him as well as
the ambassadors of the Kings of Spain and Naples,
who said to him: Be welcome!  I asked them if
they wanted to say anything more.  They answered: No.  The ambassador who head this,
added: Who does not want to say anything else
does not expect an answer.  He rode then between
the Archbishop of Cosenza, the governor of the city,
and the Archbishop of Ragusa through the Via
Papae to the inn of the Holy Apostles where he took
up his quarters.

On Monday, 31st of August, 1500, Lucretia, once
of Aragon, the daughter of the Pope, betook herself
from the city to Nepi accompanied by six hundred

on horseback in order to find some consolation and
rest after the grief and consternation in which she
had been thrown by the recent death of her husband,
Alphonse of Aragon.

On 20th December, 1500, a bull was posted on the
doors of St. Peter, concerning the prolongation of
the jubilee year until the coming feast of Epiphany
in favor of those abroad.  The Pope granted to
Italy the unlimited indulgence until the next feast
of Pentecost and nominated for this purpose as
commissaries the Minorities of the strict observance
through an Apostolic letter.

After the beginning of the last year of the jubilee
the penitentiaries of St. Peter saw from cases that
came before them in confession that the rights of indulgence granted to them were not broad enough.
In the course of a conversation I had with one of
them I asked him to let me hear some of the cases
that were submitted daily to his colleagues.  He
told me that there were varied and curious cases
reported to them but that he could not retain all of
them in his memory.  He told me, however, a few he
remembered.

Some one had concluded matrimony with a virgin
and after he had slept with her and had had intercourse with her for a certain time, he had deserted
her in order to contract a marriage with a second
and a third one.  The same he did with a fourth one
and had thus four wives living at the same time.

The same case he told me of a woman who married four men one after the other without any one of them having died.

A monk of the order of the Benedictines who had been ordained as a priest contracted a marriage with a woman and consummated it through cohabitation. They lived together for about thirty years and had six children. After the death of the woman he contracted another marriage and lived and slept with his second wife for about seven years. Then he came to the jubilee and acknowledged his error himself. Another one, who had married and had consummated the cohabitation, let himself be ordained as a priest and contracted another marriage although he had been ordained.

One had had intercourse with a woman and then married her daughter. He came to the jubilee and acknowledged his error.

A priest slept with his niece who became pregnant through him and bore him a son. The priest father christened him after his birth, then killed him immediately and buried him in the stable. Nevertheless he had celebrated mass for eighteen years after this without dispensation or rehabilitation for his deed.

Another one had taken monastic vows and entered the order of the Franciscans of the strict observance. Still within the first four months of the year of probation he left the convent, threw off the cowl and contracted a marriage with a married woman whom he later deserted after intercourse. Now he entered another order which he left within the probationary year in order to contract a marriage with another married woman. When he heard after cohabitation with her that she was the wife of some one else he left her and married another free woman with whom he also cohabited. He ran away from this one too and married a fourth one with whom he also cohabited. Finally he deserted the fourth one also and entered the order of Santa Maria of the Teutons, of which he confessed to be a member. When the fourth one heard of this she went to the convent in the belief that he was her husband and demanded his surrender. He fled before the imminent danger and came to Rome with the request to render him appropriate aid. It was said that the case was known in Strasburg.

The two principals of a merchant firm in Provins, Pierre and Jean, had both beautiful wives. Pierre, acting on information from his servants, told his wife, that he would go on a certain day to Bruges so that she could make an appointment with Jean. On that day Pierre pretended to set forth on a journey but went instead to the house of a friend and arranged with his servants that they should let him know as soon as Jean had shut up himself with his wife. This they faithfully did. Pierre then went to his house and knocked violently at the door.

The frightened wife locked the naked Jean into a chest in her room. Pierre was admitted, went to his wife's chamber and sent immediately for Jean's wife, who appeared soon afterwards. He asked her about her husband and she answered she did not know where he was. He often left the house early in the morning and returned in the late evening. Often he would stay away for one or two days. Pierre said: "Your husband is locked up in this chest here and he has often slept with my wife, although you are much more beautiful than she is. I give you the choice, either you surrender yourself to me on the top of this chest or you will see your husband cruelly murdered." The woman asked her husband in the chest what she should do. He answered from the chest that one could more easily compromise with decency than with death. So Pierre took Jean's wife on the top of the chest, then he let him out and they were the best friends. The incident had been kept secret for years.

A similar case happened in Lübeck. Philip had a very beautiful sister, and Anton whom she loved very much slept with her. She climbed through the window of her chamber over the roof and went to the room of her lover. When Philip found out that his sister had gone to Anton he sent for the sister of Anton who came to his room without any hesitation. Philip said to her: "Your brother Anton has often slept with my sister and now they are lying together again. I decided to lie with you or your brother will die an evil death." She consented in order to free her brother. After he had lain with her, he sent her back to her house through the window over the roof the same way by which his sister usually returned. When Anton heard of it, he came to an understanding with Philip that the matter should be kept secret. Nevertheless it came finally to our knowledge.

When Angelo went through a church at noon, he cast a glance into the chapel of St. Florence situated in a corner. There he saw how Grada was lying under Paolo and how they amused themselves together. For this Angelo later on reproached Paolo in public. Paolo denied the incident stubbornly, and as Angelo did not cease his pointed remarks, he sued him for libel before the magistrate. Proceedings were started against Angelo and his insults were proven while he could not justify his accusation. Judgment was rendered therefore against Angelo that he had to recant his abuse and libellous speeches publicly in the church from the pulpit and to restore the good reputation of Paolo. When therefore, on a Sunday, the principal of the church came down from the pulpit after the sermon, Angelo stepped up and told before all the people of his trial before the magistrate and of the decision rendered and recanted the abuse and libellous speeches by admitting his error in appropriate words. Then, how-

ever, he added at the end: " But as a matter of fact,
my dear co-citizens, when I saw that woman lying
on the floor and Paolo above her and her nakedness
exposed and what they were doing together just as
one is acting usually in performing the fleshly act,
then I was firmly convinced that they had performed
this act." So this last error proved to be still
worse for Paolo then the one before.

On Whitsunday, 30th May, 1500, the Pope appeared wearing the tiara under the canopy in the
procession in St. Peter's. Before the rails of the
main altar all the prelates laid down their vestments
and put on their coats as did likewise the cardinals
after the Pope had said the creed together with the
officiating cardinal. The Pope ascended the throne
and the cardinals in their coats made the obeisance
in the usual way. Cardinal Pallavicini celebrated
the mass. The Pope had ordered the evening before
that the procession of the clergy should pass before
the railing. Since, however, the Cardinal Carafa
had told the Pope this morning that at the election
of the former master of the order of the Predicants
and of another of the Minorites during the time of
Pope Sixtus IV the procession of the order with the
elected general had come to the main altar, the Pope
allowed it on this day also.

After the beginning of the epistle the procession
of the others who preceded the aforesaid order, had
passed the railing and had turned on its way to the

Vatican. The procession of the brethren, however, passed through the railing and around the main altar between the cardinal who was officiating and the other bishops and cardinals. Then they passed out through the side door towards the Vatican. Many of the brethren threw themselves down between the altar and the Pope and, turning towards the latter, they kissed the floor after the manner of the Turks. As I considered this improper, I intervened in order to prevent the others from doing so. The Pope however disapproved of my intervention and ordered that I should let them kiss the floor, which I did. The new general of the Predicants together with many provincial brethren of his order went up to the Pope, and with him Cardinal Carafa, who recommended his cause to the Pope. All the brethren kissed the foot of the Pope and then joined the procession again, the remainder of which did not pass through the railing after the general but turned toward the Vatican.

In the meanwhile Petrus of Vicenza, auditor of the Camera and Bishop of Cesena, donned a red pluviale and the plain mitre and went up to the altar to the Pope and kissed his knees. He asked, without mentioning the benediction, for the plenary indulgence which the Pope granted to all those present. After having received the indulgence he mounted the pulpit and announced in an oration the alliance between the Pope, the King of Hungary and the Signory of Venice against the Turks. He did not enter, however, into a specification and announcement of the various points. Immediately after this oration he announced the indulgence obtained from the Pope. The latter rose immediately from his throne and began without the mitre *Te Deum laudamus* in a clear voice which was continued to the end by the choir.

Then the Pope, still standing, recited the Lord's prayer as well as the verses and two prayers that have been provided for in the ceremonial at the announcement of an alliance against the infidels. Then he administered the benediction to the people as usual, stepped down and after a prayer before the altar took up the tiara and left the railing. He looked at the iron of the spear of Christ and then at the Lord's image and returned as usual to the palace.

In the evening the main bell of the Capitol was rung and bonfires were lighted throughout the city. By order of the Pope it was announced publicly in the city on the 3rd or 4th of June that all bandits and those outlawed on account of murder, theft, or other crimes could enter the city free and without punishment.

# XII

## FEASTS AND FEUDS IN ROME

ON Thursday, the 17th of June, 1501, Cardinal Borgia entered Rome about one o'clock in the night through the Porta del Popolo. His own brother, who did not belong to the clergy but was captain of the portal of the papal palace, had ridden out about two miles beyond the Milvian bridge to meet him. He did not dismount, however, when he offered him his hand. Furthermore Cardinal Lopez went out for a mile to meet him. The latter wanted Borgia to ride on the right side which was quite against the wish of Borgia. So Lopez rode on the right side and Borgia on the left, which was improper. Before the steps of the church del Popolo, Lopez remained mounted on his mule, took leave from Borgia and returned to the palace.

Borgia went into the church and from there to the rooms prepared for him. There I wanted that the barber cut his hair that hung two fingers broad over his ears and enlarged his tonsure which was small and badly done. The cardinal replied that his hair and tonsure were in order. I did not want to reply anything. As I saw his indignation, I left

him as he was and went away before Cardinal Lopez
came to him.   In the meadows we took off from the
cardinal the cape and the violet cloak of rather
thick cloth which we appropriated for ourselves as
usual.

On the same evening, about twelve o'clock in the
night, Cesare Borgia came secretly to Rome and
took up his quarters in the Vatican without being noticed by anybody.

On the following Friday, 13th June, 1501, I went
quite early in the morning to Santa Maria del Popolo, and as the chapel in the convent was too damp
and close, I decorated the chapter before the chapel
with a few orange branches as well as I could.   For
the stewards had not sent anything although they
had been requested to.   The cardinals of the palace
appeared first, and when all had assembled, Carafa
desired that we should start immediately which was
done accordingly and we mounted our horses.
There appeared still the Cardinals Orsini and
Medici, and when we had reached the hospital of the
Slavonians, Cardinal Sanseverino.   Cardinal Castro
was with the Pope in the palace.   The new cardinal
had come alone in a coat of crimson-colored camlet
while all the others were in violet ones.   He rode in
the last rank between Piccolomini at the right and
Medici at the left.   I did not send the two deacons
in advance to the Pope to dress him because I
doubted that he had arisen.   The new cardinal re-

mained with Piccolomini and Farnese in the little
chapel which was decorated with tapestry but had
no carpets on the floor. When the Pope came from
his chamber in the Camera Papagalli to don the
paraments, he reproached me for having come with
the others in such a hurry from Maria del Popolo.
I answered truly that it was after nine o'clock.

The Pope in his robes appeared at the public consistory which was held in the third hall. Four reports were given, the first by Justinus, the second
one by Burgundus. During this I conducted the
Cardinal Medici to the small chapel and sent Farnese back to the consistory. The latter bowed before the Pope and took his seat. Soon afterwards
appeared the new one with the two old cardinals at
the session. First Piccolomini, behind him the new
cardinal, rendered to the Pope the usual obeisance.
Medici remained below before the throne of the Pope.
Piccolomini and the new cardinal then stepped down
again, and the new one was greeted by all the cardinals with the kiss on the mouth. He took his seat
behind Farnese. Burgundus continued his report,
then Alphonsus Ricenas made the third and Franciscus Gerona the fourth one. After this the two
assisting cardinals went up again with the new one
to the Pope, who received also the retainers of the
new cardinal in the ceremony of kissing his foot,
while all the cardinals and prelates were sitting
around in their seats as before. Then the Pope rose

and returned to the Camera Papagalli where he laid
off the sacred robes.  On this occasion the Cardinal Pallavicini asked me in the circle why the new
cardinal alone was wearing the red coat and I answered that he did so in order not to look as if he
were of a religious order.  For Cardinal Borgia is a
knight of St. John.  Carafa and Pallavicini smiled
as they knew about this.  Finally all the cardinals
accompanied the new cardinal to the room of the
treasurer prepared for him and took leave of him.

On the same day after dinner it was announced
in Rome: that under penalty of a fine of a hundred
ducats all orders of the twenty-six so-called pro-
visors appointed by the Pope had to be obeyed.
Their task was to procure supplies for the French
soldiers who had come to conquer the kingdom of
Naples and had been quartered outside the walls.
Whoever had carts or sumpters or mules must notify
the governor of Rome in order that they could be
used to transport these supplies.  Under penalty of
two hundred ducats and forfeiture of the object no
one should dare to buy anything from the soldiers.
This was done because the latter during their advance had stolen horses, donkeys, corn and grain and
anything they could lay hands to.

On the following Saturday, 19th June, 1501, another proclamation was issued in Rome according to
which all the men of the King of France, who did not
receive pay from him or the Pope or from Cesare

Borgia, and the other soldiers in Rome who were not under the leadership of any of the afore-named should leave the city during Saturday. Whoever should be found afterwards in Rome would be punished through judgment of the governor with prison, torture, and finally also to permanent servitude at the galleys.

On the same day Monsignore de Allegri entered the city but was not received with public honors.

A place near Aqua Traversa, beyond the Milvian Bridge, was designated as a camp for the French. There pens were erected and numerous arbors clad with foliage, hundred-fifty barrels of wine were put up, provision had been made for bread, meat, eggs, cheese, fruit and everything necessary as well as for sixteen prostitutes for the requirements of the soldiers. Tradesmen and artisans of every description were ordered there for work. The governor issued the order to the Florentine merchants who dwelt on the bridge that they should according to the size of their houses prepare quarters for two, three or four mounted noblemen of the forces. The merchants wanted to get rid of this burden and gave the governor two hundred ducats which he took gladly. But when the soldiers entered the city he forced the merchants nevertheless to receive the persons designated without giving back the two hundred ducats.

On Tuesday, the 22nd of June, 1501, Cardinal Francesco Borgia went from Rome into the territory of the Colonna in order to take possession of Rocca di Papa and all the lands and castles of the Colonna in the name of the Pope. He had Papal commissaries and soldiers with him and took possession of everything without any protest or resistance.

On Wednesday, the 23rd of June, 1501, the Arch deacon of Aquila, Franciscus Lucentinus, was attacked near Pellegrino and mortally wounded by four men of Hiernoymus Gaglioffi of Aquila, his mortal enemy, of whom one had himself warned Franciscus a few days before that he would slay him with his associates if it had to be even in the house of Cardinal Piccolomini. There the dying man was brought on the same day and expired after vespers. In the evening he was carried to the church of the Saint Maria de Consolazione where he had desired to be buried and there he was interred. May he rest in peace. Amen!

On the same day the Knight Berauld Stuart d'Aubigny, Captain of the French soldiers made his entry into Rome from the direction of the meadows and was greeted in the usual way by the suites of the Pope and of all the cardinals. He rode between the Bishops Valdoes of Zamora and Pistachio of Conversano straight to the Vatican where he met the Pope in the Camera Papagalli, together with the Cardinals Pallavicinia, San Giorgio, Lopez, Ferrari and the referendaries. There he was admitted by the Pope to the ceremony of kissing his foot and

after him ten or twelve of his suite. The Pope
jested with him for a short while and dismissed him
then whereupon he, accompanied by Archbishop Sacchis of Ragusa and the Bishop Valdoes and the others who had received him, rode back to the house of
the Vice-chancellor where quarters had been provided for him. There were also present the French
ambassador, Bishop Gubé of Tréguier, the English
ambassador, and the ambassadors of the duke of
Savoy and of Venice and Florence who kept no order as the Savoyard who rode at the left of the
English ambassador was quarreling with the Venetian who rode at his right. I did not want to in-
tervene and everything else was as usual.

On the 25th or 26th of June, 1501, in the early
morning it was publicly proclaimed in the city by
order of the Pope or the governor that all those who
were not in pay of the Pope, the King of France, or
of Cesare Borgia should leave the city within three
hours and should not enter again. There was furthermore a proclamation issued in the name of the
Lord Captain d'Aubigny, that all soldiers under the
command of the King of France should stay during
the whole day in the camp assigned to them near
Aqua Traversa under penalty.

On Monday, the 28th of June, 1501, all the soldiers camping near Aqua Traversa marched through
the meadows into the Borgo Petri by order of the
Pope. There they met with all the other soldiers of

the King of France in Rome and when all were together they marched in rank and file over the bridge
of San Angelo towards Naples in execution of their
orders.   The Pope was in the castle of San Angelo
in the rooms adjoining the garden or in the loggia
from which he viewed them with great pleasure while
they marched past.   Those on foot were twelve
thousand men strong, the cavalry, two thousand.
After the soldiers there came twenty-six carriages
with thirty-six bombards.

On Tuesday, the 6th of July, 1501, a Spanish
prostitute, Ludovica, who had her quarters near the
White Fountain, was arrested, brought to the Sa-
bellian jail where she was immediately subjected to
torture and strung up within an hour.   She had
robbed her visitors as best she could and had had
several stabbed to death.   She was arrested because
a Frenchman from whom she had stolen twelve Scudi
quarreled with her in public on that account just
as the governor was passing and complained about
her to the governor.

On the 26th of July, 1501, about the fifth hour of
the night the Pope received the news of the capture
of Capua by the Duke of Valentinois.   The capture
of this city was achieved through treason by a certain Fabrizio, a citizen of Capua, who let the men
of the Duke enter in secret.   But Fabrizio himself
was the first one to be killed by them and after him
there were about three thousand soldiers on foot and

two hundred horsemen slain as well as citizens, priests, monks and nuns in churches and covents, and women as many as there were found of them, without any pity. And the girls that were captured were given as a prey to the soldiers who treated them with great cruelty. The number of all that were killed has been estimated at about four thousand.

On the morning of the 27th July, 1501, the Pope went from Rome to Sermoneta and the places of the Colonnas with fifty horsemen and a hundred soldiers on foot, in the midst of all his confidential retainers and the cardinals who accompanied him. With him rode the Cardinals Serra and Borgia, each of them with twelve servants, who are comprised in the aforesaid hundred-and-fifty. The Pope took luncheon in the castle Gandolfo and afterwards went down to the lake where he amused himself during the whole day in a gondola while his men shouted continuously Borgia! Borgia! firing off their blunderbusses.

On the following Thursday the Pope rode to Rocca di Papa and returned in the evening during a heavy rain-storm to the castle Gandolfo. On Friday, the 30th of July, he went again through torrents and storm to Genzano. On Saturday, the last of July, he proceeded in the same weather from Genzano to Sermoneta. Before leaving Rome he handed over his room, the whole palace, and the current affairs to his daughter Lucretia, who also occupied the papal rooms during his absence. He charged her also to open the letters sent him, and, in case any difficulty should arise, to consult Cardinal Costa and the other cardinals whom she might call upon for that purpose.

It is said that at one occasion Lucretia sent for Costa and explained the order of the Pope and a pending case. Costa considered the case as being without importance and said to Lucretia that when the Pope brought up these affairs before the consistory there was the Vice-chancellor or another cardinal who kept the record for him. It would be proper therefore if there were some one present who would note down the conversation. Lucretia answered: "I understand quite well how to write!" Costa asked: "Where is your pen?" Lucretia understood the meaning and joke of the cardinal. She smiled and they brought the conversation to an end in good humor. I was not consulted about these matters.

On Friday, the 13th of August, 1501, early in the morning a placard was hung upon the statue of Master Pasquino at the corner of the house of Carafa announcing the death of the Pope if he should leave the city. This spread immediately throughout Rome and the same morning similar posters were hung up in various parts of the city containing the following words:

I said to you before, O Pope, you were an ox;
I tell you now, you die, if you go out;
The wheel will follow him who drove the ox.[1]

On Saturday, the 4th of September, 1501, about vespers the news came from Ferrara of the conclusion of the marriage contract between Alphonso, the first-born of the Duke of Ferrara and Lucretia Borgia. Therefore bombards were set off continuously from the castle of San Angelo from then until into the night. On the following Sunday after breakfast Lucretia rode from the palace where she resided to the church Santa Maria del Popolo, dressed in a robe of golden brocade accompanied by about three hundred on horseback. Before her rode four bishops, namely Hieronymus de Porcarris, Vincenz Pistachio, Petrus Gamboa, and Antonio Flores, two by two. Then followed Lucretia alone and after her her suite and servants. In the same way she returned to the palace.

On the same day the main bell of the Capitol was rung from the hour of supper until the third hour in the night. Numerous fires were lighted in the castle of San Angelo and over the whole city. The towers of the castle and the Capitol and others were illuminated in order to excite everybody to joy, though shame would have been more fitting.

[1] The ox is an allusion to the Borgia arms, a bull pasant on a field, and the wheel to the arms of the Cardinal of Lisbon.

On the following Monday two jugglers, to one of whom on horseback Donna Lucretia had given her new robe of brocade worn only once on the previous day and worth three hundred ducats, went through all the main streets and alleys of Rome with the loud cry: " Long live the noble Duchess of Ferrara, long live Pope Alexander! Long may they live." And then the other one on foot to whom Donna Lucretia had also given a robe went along with the same cry.

On Thursday, the 9th of September, 1501, there was hung at the wall of the Torre di Nona a woman who had stabbed her husband to death with a knife during the previous night.

On Saturday, the 25th of September, the Pope went early in the morning to Nepi, Civita Castellana, and to the other places in the neighborhood, and with him Cesare Borgia and the Cardinals Serra, Francesco and Ludovico Borgia with a small suite. Donna Lucretia remained in the chamber of the Pope in order to guard it and with the same orders as upon the previous absence of the Pope. He returned to Rome on Saturday, the 23rd of October, 1501.

On the evening of the last day of October, 1501, Cesare Borgia arranged a banquet in his chambers in the Vatican with fifty honest prostitutes, called courtesans, who danced after the dinner with the attendants and the others who were present, at first in their garments, then naked. After the dinner the candelabra with the burning candles were taken from the tables and placed on the floor, and chestnuts were strewn around, which the naked courtesans picked up, creeping on hands and knees between the chandeliers, while the Pope, Cesare, and his sister Lucretia looked on. Finally prizes were announced for those who could perform the act most often with the courtesans, such as tunics of silk, shoes, barrets, and other things.

On Monday, the 11th of November, 1501, there entered the city through the Porta Viridarii a peasant leading two mares laden with wood. When these arrived in the place of St. Peter the men of the Pope ran towards them and cut the saddle-bands and ropes, and throwing down the wood they led the mares to the small place that is inside the palace just behind the portal. There four stallions freed from reins and bridles were sent from the palace and they ran after the mares and with a great struggle and noise fighting with tooth and hoof jumped upon the mares and covered them, tearing and hurting them severely. The Pope stood together with Donna Lucretia under the window of the chamber above the portal of the palace and both looked down at what was going on there with loud laughter and much pleasure.

## XIII

## CLOSING YEARS OF ALEXANDER'S REIGN

ON the evening of the 5th of January, 1502, as I have been told, the Pope counted out a hundred thousand ducats in minted gold in the presence of the brothers of the bridegroom, Ferdinand and Sigismund, as a dowry for Donna Lucretia, which he paid over to them in coined money. While counting out the money he received a letter from France according to which the French King had restored full liberty to the cardinal Ascanio Sforza.

To-day, on the 6th of January, Donna Lucretia started on her journey from the Vatican to her husband in Ferrara. She rode straightway to the Bridge of San Angelo, from there to the left past the house of the former Cardinal of Parma through the Porta del Popolo. In her retinue she had about six horses, and she wore no luxurious garments. The order of the outriders was the usual one including the armed guards. Behind them rode the Cardinal Francesco Borgia whom the Pope had recently named papal legate *de latere* in order to conduct Donna Lucretia through the territory of the Church. He rode between Don Ferdinand at the

157

right and Don Sigismund at the left. Then came
Donna Lucretia between the Cardinal d'Este at the
right and Cesare Borgia at the left, and behind them
their men in rank and file. There was no bishop,
prothonotary or abbot in the train, but instead the
papal shield-bearers and Roman nobles, who accompanied Lucretia on their own account. They all
had on new garments of gold and silver brocades
and divers silken stuffs made for the occasion. Furthermore the Pope had during these days requested
the cardinals through my colleague that each of
them should lend three horses or mules and he had
also asked many bishops, more than twenty in number, that they should each put one stallion or one
steed at the disposal of the escort of Lucretia to
Ferrara which they did. A few cardinals, however,
contributed only a single horse or mule and none of
the borrowed animals was ever returned.

The other day, before the Cardinal d'Este came
to Rome with his suite, the Pope bethought him of
his own will to honor those who had appeared with
him in addition to his servants, and were to make
the journey to Ferrara with Donna Lucretia, and
distributed the new arrivals with their attendants
among the houses of those who belonged to the *curia*.
To each cleric of the Camera he assigned twelve persons and twelve horses and the same number to the
clerics of the collegium, and to the other officials a
certain number, to each alike. Every one had to

bear the whole expense of entertaining the guests who were quartered upon him except for the partial contribution that the Pope or the *Apostolic Camera* made per man and beast. Furthermore it was said that the Pope extended the carnival in Ferrara to the eve of Laetare Sunday, so that they could eat meat in the meantime without penance, and could hold celebrations and make merry in honor of the arrival of Donna Lucretia.

During the night of Friday, the 27th of January, 1502, the brother of Signor Giovanni Lorenzo of Venice was arrested, who is said to have translated into Latin and sent to Venice a pamphlet against the Pope and Cesare Borgia written in Greek by the said Giovanni. During this night his whole goods and belongings, including those Giovanni had left behind, books and other things were dragged out of his house and nothing was left within. This was reported immediately to the Signoria of Venice, which wrote back and instructed its ambassador to make representations to the Pope with a view to his liberation. In pursuance of this instruction the ambassador presented the letter together with the request for his liberation to the Pope on Monday, the 31st of January.

The Pope is said to have answered that he had not realized that this matter was one of such great interest to the Signoria and consequently it was a matter of regret to him to be unable to grant their request for the reason that he for whom they petitioned had already been disposed of. For according to report he had been strangled as the Pope came back to Rome and thrown into the Tiber.

On the 1st of March, 1502, the Pope and his son, Cesare Borgia, had gone on a pleasure trip, each on his own ship with his suite.

On Sunday, the 5th of March, the two ships continued their journey in spite of the stormy sea and weather to Corneto in the neighborhood of which they put in. The Duke, apprehending greater danger, left the ship at the dinner hour, entered a small boat and rowed for the shore. There he sent to Corneto for horses and rode to the city. The Pope, however, was not able to make the harbor with his ship, whereupon all on board were stricken with fear, and frightened by the stormy sea cast themselves down here and there on the floor of the boat.

The Pope alone remained sitting firm and unafraid in his armchair on the quarterdeck and looked on at everything, and when the wild seas dashed against the ship, he said: " Jesus! " and crossed himself. He frequently addressed the sailors, ordering them to prepare food for the meal. But they excused themselves on the plea that they were unable to make any fire on account of the disturbed sea and the continuous tempest. When after a time the sea had subsided somewhat they fried fishes which the Pope ate. On the evening of this Saturday the Pope returned by ship with his whole retinue to Porto Ercole and sent the same night to Corneto for riding accommodations which arrived on the following Sunday.

On Thursday, the 9th of June, 1502, there was found in the Tiber strangled with a cross-bow around his neck the Signor of Faenza, a young man of about 18 years, and of such handsome figure and appearance that his like could hardly have been found among a thousand young men of his age. There were also found two young people bound to each other by the arms, the one fifteen years of age and the other twenty-five years, and with them a woman and many others.

On Sunday, the 3rd of July, 1502, a strong rope was stretched in that court of the Vatican where the Cardinals usually dismount from their horses, four or five rods above the ground and ten to twelve rods long. Upon this rope a man-at-arms of Alphonso d'Este, the husband of Lucretia, gave a performance carrying a boy on his shoulders and exhibited various other feats of rope-dancing. The Pope looked on with many cardinals, prelates and others as spectators.

On the same Sunday at about seven o'clock there passed away in the convent of Minerva at the age of almost hundred years a friar, George Alemanus of Steiermark, of the third order of the Dominicans. The monks give numerous examples of his praiseworthy and religious life, asserting that he went straight to heaven. They laid him in his cowl on a bier before the high altar of the church of the convent. And there he lay stretched out straight while during his lifetime he had gone around bowed over and very bent. He lay in this state the following Monday and Tuesday until vespers when he was lifted up on the bier before the altar. The people trooped by in masses and there was a mighty throng. Many friars stood near the bier around the altar as a guard against the crowd. I also saw him. He was well preserved and had no odor of putrefaction. Many miracles are said to have been worked on the lame and the sick, whom he restored to health, but I could not discover anything reliable. When the Pope heard of the matter he ordered him to be buried during the night of Wednesday, which took place in the presence of the *bargello* of the city.

On Wednesday, the 6th of July, 1502, at nine o'clock in the morning a cleric of the diocese of Basle by the name of Hieronymus was placed with the cap of infamy on his head on a wooden ladder which was propped against the columns of benediction on the steps of Saint Peter before the place of audience. He had confessed that he had signed and dated eleven petitions with the name of the Cardinals Pallvicini and San Giorgio and with the inscription on the back: " Registrata," and furthermore with the book and page of the register of promotions for

the holy ordinations.  He had also added the name
of the cleric of the camera as though they had been
admitted by him to the ordinations.

Thus the auditor of the Camera told to me and
many others the same morning.  At his feet a peasant was stationed also with a cap of disgrace for
having borne false witness.  And so they stood until
the end of the consistorium and the audience which
lasted about five hours.

On Tuesday, the 12th of July, the Cardinal
d'Albret and François Troches returned to Rome
with their mistresses as secretly as they had departed, without having executed their order to ap-
prehend the Cardinal Giuliano delle Rovere because
the Lord protected him from the hands of the im-
pious.

On Wednesday, the 20th of July, 1502, at nine
o'clock Giovanni Battista de Ferrari, Cardinal of
Modena and Capua, delivered his soul to the guardian of Orcus in his apartment in the Vatican.  He
was taken sick on Sunday, the 3rd of July, and did
not allow himself to be bled nor to have an enema
administered, nor did he take any syrups, pills or
any other medicine.  Instead on the fourth or fifth
day of his sickness he had a bread soup made with a
cup of the best Corsican wine.  He ate this and
drank the wine.

On Wednesday, the 10th of July, 1502, he made
confession and received the sacrament of the Eucha-

rist. On this day a fever resulting from two intermittent fevers which was very violent and which he had in addition to his constant fever, stopped and only appeared again on Saturday, the 16th. He had several capable physicians who visited him constantly but they could not persuade him to take any medicine until Sunday, the 17th, when he took one-sixth or eighth of the medicine prescribed which only served to hurt more than help him. Nor did he want to make any will or choose any burial place or make any bequests or gifts to his servants. On the morning before his death, perhaps in the delirium, he complained that somebody with whom he had made arrangements for a petition had cheated him to the extent of ten ducats. Two monks were present who remarked this. They brought him back to consciousness, held the crucifix before him and said: "Venerable Lord, do not worry about arrangements, but take your refuge to this, entrust yourself to Him who will redeem you from all fraud and deception." Thereupon he kissed the crucifix, touched his lip and made the sign of contrition. Soon afterwards he breathed forth his spirit. May he rest in peace!

The same morning a secret consistorium was held, at which the Pope transferred the church of Capua which had become vacant through the death of Ferrari to the Cardinal d'Este. As the head of the church of Modena he appointed the brother of the deceased, Don Francesco de Ferrari, an uncouth man and a layman, who had come to Rome on Monday, the 18th, at the news of the illness of his brother, the Cardinal. In order to receive the church of the deceased Cardinal he had spent all his own money in bribery for this purpose and had also renounced the whole estate of his brother.

The elected was clothed, immediately after the conclusion of the consistorium, in the ecclesiastical robes in which he appeared to us like a monster. On account of my former acquaintance with him I gave him my hand in order to congratulate him. He took it and was for kissing it if I had not withdrawn my hand.

The Pope charged my colleague and ordered that the same arrangements should be made for his funeral as had been made upon the death of the Cardinal of Capua, who had died on the 15th of August of the previous year. In his anteroom we prepared a bier, on which we laid the dead at six o'clock adorned with all the priestly vestments which had been newly made for him from violet taffeta. At the right and the left six torches were set up. Here he lay until nine o'clock. Neither the Cardinals nor their suites nor other clerics were invited into the palace. The clergy of Saint Peter's awaited him with the cross in the outer hall of the church. The beneficiaries of Saint Peter's bore the dead from his chamber to the place of the burial, preceded by thirty torch-bearers. The Responsorium was sung in the customary manner in the center of the church. He was then carried to the chapel of Santa Maria delle Febbri where he was to be interred.

All torches were taken away and I retained but one with difficulty to lighten the funeral. One of his confidential men threw himself upon the corpse and drew a ring off his hand, which the dead Cardinal had bought for two carlines. He also took an old wallet from him which was worth hardly two carlines and which the same confidential man had received from the papal sacristy with the promise to give it back again.

The coffin was somewhat too small; therefore a carpenter kneeled on the corpse to force it in. He was buried barely two spans deep below the floor besides the wall and the outer pavement between the altar of Santa Maria delle Febbri and the altar of Pope Calixtus III. For a few days the place of burial was without a sign nor were there any torches placed on it as was the custom with cardinals.

Finally this was done by the beneficiaries of Saint Peter's, to whom fifty carlines were paid according to agreement for carrying the corpse. The tomb looked for a few days like the grave of one who had been hanged, for some rascals had scratched two gallows on it and had engraved above the one from which a rope hung down, the words: " The Lord will demand the intercessions from your hands and you will have to account for them. If you cannot you will be tortured with eternal punishment."

Because he was severe against the poor and altogether too cruel and frequently of the utmost hardness toward all, and sold the livings and offices as dearly as he could in order to please the people, he had brought upon himself general despite and contempt. Several people had therefore made epitaphs to his inglorious memory, twenty-seven of which came into my hands.[1]

I was also told that there had been found one morning a placard affixed at the outer door of the apartments of the deceased cardinal in the Vatican upon which were inscribed the words: *Bos bona, terra corpus, Styx animam.* ("The ox the goods, the earth the body, the Styx the soul.") Furthermore it was said, that a Frenchman had told the following story in the servants' room of the Archbishop Sacchis de Ragusa. Ferrari appeared before the portal of heaven and knocked, petitioning to enter the realm of God. Peter asked then: "Who is knocking there?" He answered: "He from Modena." Whereupon Peter replied: "If you do not pay a thousand ducats, you cannot en-

[1] The following is a specimen of one of these pasquinades:

Iron-made was my family called, but golden
    through me,
And the cause of this was not virtue but
    robbery.

ter the realm of God." Modena, answered: "I have no money." Thereupon Peter: "Then give me five hundred." The answer was: "I have neither thousand nor five hundred. Poor I departed from life, robbed of all my possessions, livings, money, gold and silver vessels, and all my riches have been taken by the Pope. Naked I come; in the name of God have pity upon me." Peter went down step by step from five hundred to one ducat, which he wanted to levy as admission from him. But when Ferrari continued to advance the pretext of his poverty, Peter told him: "If you cannot even pay one ducat, go to the devil and stay poor with him to all eternity."

The Frenchman thus alluded to the life and conduct of Ferrari who extorted money from the poor with great cruelty. He had pity for none, but sent the poor always to the devil, to enjoy eternal poverty with him. That is also why Peter above consigned him to the eternal fire of hell. So Ferrari comes to hell and knocks there. The doorkeeper asks who knocks. He receives the answer: "He from Modena." The doorkeeper bargains in the same way about the price. And as Ferrari was not ready to pay anything, he drove him away and assigned him a place aside where he should be tormented with eternal punishment.

I feel deeply grieved in soul that he had been so cruel to the poor and had bethought himself so little of the welfare of his soul, while he showed toward me only munificence, generosity and appreciation. May Almighty God have mercy upon his soul. He is reported to have left thirty thousand double ducats in coined money, ten thousand in other coin, and gold and silver vessels to the value of ten thousand ducats. That he left so many ducats, I hardly believe.

On the first day of Christmas, 1502, thirty masked men with long thick noses in the form of enormous phalli proceded after dinner to the place of Saint Peter. Before them a cardinal's chest was born, to which was affixed a shield with three dice. Then came the masked fellows and behind them some one rode in a long coat and an old cardinal's hat. The fellows rode also on donkeys, some of them on such small ones that their feet touched the ground and that they walked thus astride together with the donkeys. They went up to the little place between the portal of the palace and the hall of audience, where they showed themselves to the Pope who stood at the window above the portal in the Loggia Paulina. Then they made a procession through the whole city.

At two o'clock on the night of the 3rd of January, 1503, the Pope made known to the Cardinal Orsini and to Jacobus de Santa Croce that Cesare Borgia had now taken the Castle of Sinigaglia. Therefore, in order to congratulate the Pope, the cardinal rode in the morning to the Vatican, and with him the governor of the city who made as if he accompanied him by accident. After the cardinal had alighted in the palace, all his horses and mules were brought to the papal stables and he found himself suddenly surrounded by armed men in the Camera Papagalli and fainted. He was brought immediately to the Torre di Nona prison, behind the garden or arbor of the Pope into the room of the Bishop Gamboa and with him afterwards the Protonotary Orsini, Jacobus de Santa Croce, and the Abbot Bernardo de Alvino who were all kept there in confinement.

The secretary and treasurer of the Pope, Adriano Castelli, who had on the preceding night read the letter of Cesare to the Pope in which he notified the Pope that he should arrest the Cardinal Orsini and Jacobus in the morning, did not want to leave the papal chamber that night so that if the Cardinal Orsini should be warned, the Pope might not suspect that he had done it.

The same Adriano sent for the Archbishop Rinaldo Orsini of Florence on the morning that the cardinal rode to the Vatican and had him arrested and placed under guard in his room in the Vatican. After the arrest of the cardinal the governor rode with all his men to his house on the Monte Giordano, locked it, placed guards before it and took up his residence there himself. While this was happening in Rome, Cesare had apprehended in Sinigaglia, Vitelozzo Vitelli, Paolo Orsini, Don Francesco, Duke de Gravina . . . and Liberotto . . . de Ferma,[1] and of these he caused Vitelozzo and Liberotto to be strangled within a few hours by Michelotto; the Duke de Gravina, Paolo and Don Francesco he kept under strict guard.

The son of Paolo, Fabio Orsini, prudently fled with all possible haste, when he saw the arrest of his father and the others. After the apprehension of the Cardinal Orsini, the rumor spread in Rome that the Pope was dead and that Naples had been taken by the Spaniards, but there was nothing in it. When the Cardinal Cesarini heard of the arrest of the Cardinal Orsini, he had his bell rung as a signal for riding away, and without delay he mounted his mule and rode in all haste through highways and byways to the Vatican. He remained there a short while but soon wearied of this he returned to his residence as he had come.

This day and the following night Carlo Orsini was held a prisoner in the chamber of the Torre di Nona. The next day he was brought into the rooms above the main chapel and kept there under guard until vespers of the next Thursday. Then he was transferred to the Castle San Angelo where the major-domo received him in his room. The prothono-

---

[1] The dots indicate gaps in the manuscript.

tary and the abbott were brought there soon after the arrest. Jacobus de Santa Croce was kept a prisoner in the Vatican.

Cesare Borgia had seized the prisoners mentioned above in the following way. When he was lying before the Castle of Sinigaglia with Vitelozzo, Paolo and the others he pretended that he did not want yet to advance against the castle, but preferred rather to take a meal first and he invited those mentioned to partake with him. The Duke entered the house followed by Paolo, to whom he had extended a special invitation. Then came Vitelozzo, whom Paolo had caused to be called, and the others came behind them. When they were all within the courtyard, the Duke went into one of the rooms, whereupon Michelotto and many others surrounded Vitelozzo as well as Paolo, with the words: " You are under arrest." Thereupon Vitelozzo snatched out his dagger and wounded several who had thrown themselves upon him. This was in vain, for he and others were put into prison and treated as has been told.

On Wednesday, the 4th of January, Jacobus de Santa Croce engaged himself to the Pope to report at any time and place that he should desire. For this he pledged himself and his property as a bond for the fines of the papal chamber. Several citizens took a guaranty of twenty thousand ducats upon themselves and he was set at liberty on the same day and returned to his residence soon after vespers. In the evening of the same day the governor stayed in the apartment of the Archbishop Orsini of Florence and after dinner he had all possessions of the Cardinal Orsini and of the Archbishop brought in their carriages and other vehicles to the Vatican or to his own house according to his pleasure. Many things were also taken by the soldiers and others and carried away.

On Thursday, the 5th of January, 1503, the sun shone through the clouds early in the morning and then retired behind them. It did not rain until vespers, but then rain fell during the whole night and the next day.

The same morning Jacobus de Santa Croce rode with Prince Goffredo, the son of the Pope, to Monte Rotonca and in the name of the Pope took possession of it as well as of all land of the Orsini and also of the Abbey of Farfa.

At the usual hour the papal vespers were said in the main chapel. Mass was conducted with the Cardinal San Giorgio officiating. The Pope was not present. After this the cardinals went to the Pope to intercede for the Cardinal Orsini. The Pope told them of the conspiracy of Vitelozzo, of the Orsini, of Baglioni and Pandolfo and their accomplices for the assassination of Cesare Borgia, who wanted to take revenge on them. Their intercession was of no avail.

The same day the city of Perugia surrendered to the Pope. Its tyrant Giovanni Paolo had previously fled to Pandolfo in Siena.

On the 6th of January, 1503, after dinner the governor rode to the residence of the auditor of the camera, Bishop Petro Menzi of Cesena, summoned him to his presence, sick as he was, and brought him to the Castle San Angelo where he had him locked up and placed under guard. Then he went to the Vatican and from there to the residence of Andrea Spiriti of Viterbo, prothonotary of the Apostolic See and cleric of the papal camera, with whom he proceeded as he had done with Menzi. When the prothonotary realized that he had been arrested, he threw the keys of his library and his money chest into the sewer, for what reason I do not know.

The following Saturday the governor ordered all the possessions of the bishop auditor as well as of the prothonotary to be carried from his residence to the Vatican. It was said that only very little had been found in the house of the prothonotary.

Alarmed by the arrest of the auditor and the prothontary, Spiriti, the Bishop of Chiusi, Sinoflo of Castle Lotario, cleric of the Apostolic camera and papal Secretary, contracted the fever and made his will on Saturday, the 4th of January, and as executors he designed the Cardinals Pallavicini and Piccolomini. To the Pope he bequeathed a hundred ducats. Soon afterward he gave up the ghost. May he rest in peace. Amen.

When the Pope heard of his demise, he sent my colleague, Bernardino Gutterii, and one of the ushers of his chamber to the residence of the deceased to guard the house and the property within. There appeared also the Bishop Petrucci de Soana in the name of one of the executors, Piccolomini. All ecclesiastical paraments were of purple cloth newly made for the deceased. The governor came also, and he alone was admitted by the two emissaries of the Pope, but he did not touch anything.

On Wednesday, January the 18th, 1503, the Duke of Gravina, Paolo Orsini, and the Knight Orsini, who had been taken prisoner recently in Sinigaglia, were strangled by Michelotto and Marco Romano by order of Cesare Borgia at the Castle della Pieve in the territory of Siena.

On Wednesday, the 23rd of January, 1503, the report was circulated in Rome that Cesare had brought under his rule recently Chiusi and Pienza as well as the places of Sarteano, Castle della Pieve and Santo Quirico, where only two old men and nine old women were found. The men of the Duke hung them up by the arms and lighted fires beneath their soles, in order to force them through this torture to confess where property had been hidden. But they could or would not confess and perished under the torture. The villainous band tore the roofs from the houses, the beams, windows, doors, chests and barrels, from which they had let the wine run out, and set fire to everything. They took with them whatever they could plunder in the places they passed through, as well as in Aquapendente, Monte-fiascone, Viterbo, and everywhere else.

In the evening of the 1st of February, 1503, a corpse was found in the river near the Ponte Nuovo without clothing and with scarlet stockings. During these days Antonio de Pistorio and his associate were forbidden to see the Cardinal Orsini to whom they were accustomed to bring every day the food and drinks sent by his mother. This was done, as it has been said, because the Pope had requested from the cardinal two thousand ducats which a relative of the cardinal had deposited for the sale of a large pearl to him. The pearl had been bought by the cardinal himself for the price of two thousand ducats from a certain Virgilio Orsini or his heirs. In order to come to the assistance of her son, the mother of the cardinal, when she heard of it, paid the Pope the two thousand ducats, and the mistress of the cardinal, who had the said pearl, procured admission to the Pope in male attire and presented him the pearl. Possessed of the pearl and the money, the Pope gave the order that the two should be allowed again as before to bring the cardinal food and drink. The cardinal had, however, in the meantime, as the people said, emptied the cup that had been prepared for him by order and direction of the Pope.

On Thursday, the 2nd of February, 1503, the feast of Purification, the Pope blessed and distributed the candles in the main chapel without any crowding. Nevertheless he had around himself the wooden railing. Two conservators held the candles for the Pope. Cardinal Castro celebrated the solemn mass in the chapel. All this was done in the usual and customary manner.

On Monday, the 13th of February, 1503, it was said in Rome, that Giangiordano Orsini had surrendered to the Pope and Cesare without any condition, that furthermore, Pandolfo Petrucci of Siena and Gian Paolo Baglioni of Perugia had been taken prisoners on Florentine territory.

On Wednesday, the 15th of February, 1503, the Cardinal d'Este departed from Rome after the consistory in which he had taken part, in order to return to Ferrara on account of the resentment Cesare Borgia bore toward him because he loved the princely sister-in-law of Cesare and had had intercourse with her as also had had Cesare.

On Thursday, the 16th of February, the Pope sent bombards to Cesare from the Castle San Angelo to aid in reducing Bracciano.

On Monday, the 20th of February, a secret consistory was held during which the Pope told the cardinals that the Orsini were planning to invade

Rome by stealth and to pillage the houses of the cardinals. He, therefore, warned the cardinals that every one of them should lay in a store of provisions for himself in his house and protect it with artillery. He complained of Cesare that hitherto he had not been willing to obey his orders concerning the conquest of Bracciano and the other strongholds of the Orsini, but that he preferred to listen to the King of France, although he was captain of the church. He declared he would insist in any case on the capture of Bracciano and the other places. Furthermore, Cardinal Orsini had offered him 25,000 ducats for his release. He had consoled and admonished him to be of good cheer and before all to take good care of his health, since everything was of secondary importance, and he had ordered all the physicians to take the greatest care of the welfare of the cardinal.

On Wednesday, the 22nd of February, the Cardinal Orsini died in the Castle of San Angelo. May his soul rest in peace! Amen!

The Pope commanded my colleague, Bernardino Gutterii, to arrange the funeral of the deceased. I will not, therefore, attend the ceremony myself nor have anything to do with it, as I have no wish to learn aught that does not concern me.[1]

---

[1] It is highly probable that the cardinal was poisoned by order of the Borgias.

# XIV

## THE DEATH AND FUNERAL OF ALEXANDER

ON Saturday, the 12th of August, 1503, the Pope fell ill in the morning. After the hour of vespers, between six and seven o'clock a fever appeared and remained permanently.

On the 15th of August thirteen ounces of blood were drawn from him and the tertian ague supervened.

On Thursday, the 17th of August, at nine o'clock in the forenoon he took medicine.

On Friday, the 18th, between nine and ten o'clock he confessed to the Bishop Gamboa of Carignola, who then read mass to him. After his communion he gave the Eucharist to the Pope who was sitting in bed. Then he ended the mass at which were present five cardinals, Serra, Juan and Francesco Borgia, Casanova and Loris. The Pope told them that he felt very bad. At the hour of vespers after Gamboa had given him extreme unction, he died.

There were present, in addition, only the datary and the papal grooms. Cesare, who was lying sick in bed, sent Michelotto with many men, who locked all doors at the entrance to the residence of the Pope. One of them drew a dagger and threatened Cardinal Casanova, if he did not give him the keys and the money of the Pope, he would stab him and throw him out of the window, whereupon the frightened cardinal surrendered the keys to him. One after the other they entered the room behind the chamber of the Pope and took all the silver they could find as well as two chests with 100,000 ducats each. At eight o'clock they opened the doors again and the death of the Pope became known. In the meantime his servants had appropriated whatever was left in the wardrobes and they left nothing but the papal armchairs, a few cushions, and the rugs on the walls. Cesare did not appear during the whole illness of the Pope and not even at his death. Nor did the Pope mention him or Lucretia with one word.

After seven o'clock my colleague arrived at the Vatican, and was recognized and admitted. He found the Pope dead and had him washed by the servant of the sacristy, Balthasar, and a papal servant. Then they put on him all his everyday garments and a white coat without a train which he had never worn while alive. Over this they put a surplice. And thus they laid him on a bier in the ante-chamber of the hall, where he had died, with a crimson silk and a beautiful carpet over him.

After eight o'clock my colleague sent for me and I came. The cardinals in the city had not yet re-

ceived any announcement, but during the time that I
went to the Vatican, it was communicated to them.
But none of them made any move nor did they meet
anywhere else. I suggested to Carafa that he ought
to prepare for imminent dangers and after nine
o'clock he notified all the cardinals, through his secretary, that they should deign to appear the next
morning in Santa Maria Minerva. There, in the
middle of the sacristy, four benches were placed for
the cardinals in a quadrangle. When I came to the
Pope I dressed him in red robes all of brocade, with
a short fanon, a beautiful chasuble, and with stockings. And as there was no cross on the shoes, I
put on instead his daily slippers of crimson velvet
with the golden cross which I bound with two strings
to the back of the heels. His ring was missing and
I could not recover it. Thereupon we carried him
through the two rooms, the hall of the Pontiffs,
and the audience room, to the Camera Papagalli,
where we prepared a beautiful table of one rod in
length with a crimson cover and a beautiful rug
over it. We obtained four cushions of brocade and
one of crimson velvet. The one of old crimson velvet we did not use, but of the others we laid one
under the shoulders of the Pope, two besides and one
beneath the head and over this an old carpet. And
so he lay throughout the night with two torches,
quite alone, although the prothonotaries had been
invited to read the burial service.

I returned to the city during the night, after twelve o'clock, accompanied by eight palace-guards. In the name of the Vice-chancellor I ordered the runner Carlo, together with his companions, under penalty of the loss of his office, to inform the whole clergy of Rome, both regular and secular, that they should be at the Vatican on the morrow at nine o'clock in the morning to escort the body from the main chapel to St. Peter's. Two hundred torches were prepared for the escort of the Pope.

On the following Monday, the 19th of August, 1503, I had the coffin brought to the Camera Papagalli and laid the body in it. The subdeacon, in his cloak, stood ready to carry the cross, but we could not find the papal cross. The shield-bearers and a few servants of the chamber were called together to bear forty-three torches as well as four penitentiaries, namely the Bishop of Milopotamo, Claudius, Cataleni, Andreas Frisner, and Arnold de Bedietto of the order of the Minorites. During the night they sung the requiem, sitting on the window-bench and laying their hands on the bier of the Pope, which was then carried by the poor who stood around in order to see the Pope. I then put a double mattress into the coffin and over it a beautiful new bishop's cloak of brocade of pale mauve with two new veils on which were embroidered the arms of Pope Alexander. I then laid the Pope on this and covered him with an old rug and placing an old pillow beneath his shoulders and two cushions of brocade beneath his head. Two new crimson hats with golden strings I took home with me. The body thus wrapped up was borne by our servants, but they became apprehensive that they would not be able to carry it out of the palace which they were quite well, and they left it to the chaplain of the palace, the Bishop of Sessa, to guard him.

We brought the Pope to the main chapel, where the regular clergy of Rome, the clergy of St. Peter's, and the canons with the cross assembled. Then he was carried from the main chapel to the center of St. Peter's. First came the cross, then the monks of St. Onofrio, the Paulist Fathers, the Franciscans, Augustinians and Carmelites, three brethren only of the Order of the Predicants together with the clergy of St. Peter's and the chamberlain of the Roman clergy in stole and pluviale with a few priests. About a hundred-and-forty torches were borne for the most part by the clerics and beneficiaries of St. Peter's and by servants and retainers of the Pope. Then came the body. The beneficiaries and clerics surrounded the coffin without any order, and it was carried by the poor who had stood around it in the chapel, while four or six canons went beside them with their hands on the bier. Only four prelates followed the coffin, two by two, namely, the major-domo, Bishop Deza of Zamora, his vicar Gamboa, and the bishops of Narni and Sessa.

When the coffin was deposited in the center of the church, the *Non intres in judicium,* etc., should have been recited, but there was no book there. While we were waiting for it in vain, the clergy intonated the responsorium: *Libera me, Domine.* During the singing some soldiers of the palace-guard attempted to appropriate several torches. The clergy defended itself against them and the soldiers turned their weapons against the clergy, who left their singing and fled to the sacristy. And the Pope was left lying there almost alone. I took up the bier together with three others and we carried him up to the main altar and the papal throne and placed him with the head towards the altar, closing the choir behind the coffin. The bishop of Sessa feared that if the people came near to the dead, there might be a scandal, that is, some one whom the dead had injured might take revenge upon him. Therefore he had the coffin taken away again and had it deposited at the entrance of the chapel between the stairs, the feet so near to the rails and the door that one could touch them easily with the hand through the railing. There it remained the whole day through behind the well-closed railing.

In the meantime sixteen cardinals had assembled in Sta. Maria Minerva after nine o'clock. They appointed Archbishop Sachis of Ragusa as governor of Rome and assigned two hundred soldiers to him. The office of the chamberlain they handed over to

Cardinal Vera. And to these two they entrusted the supervision of the gates of Rome and of the populace and the clergy. The leaden seal of Alexander VI was broken before them in their presence by the plumbators, and they ordered that the papal ring should be handed over to the datary, which was done by Cardinal Casanova, while Pallavicini and Borgia charged themselves with the task of taking an inventory of the possessions of the Pope in his chamber. The congregation ended about three o'clock.

After dinner the cardinals before named, together with the clerics of the Camera, took an inventory of the silver and costly furnishings. They found the papal crown and two precious tiaras, all the rings which the Pope used at the mass, and the whole service of vessels used by the Pope when officiating, as much as could be packed into eight large chests. There were furthermore silver vessels in the first chamber behind the papal apartment, which Michelotto Neri had overlooked, and a box of cyprus wood which was covered with a green cloth and had also not been discovered. In this box were precious stones and rings to the value of about twenty-five thousand ducats, many papers, among them the oath of the cardinals, the bull of investiture of the kingdom of Naples and various other documents.

The cleric of the chamber, Fernando Ponzetto, made arrangements during my absence with the carpenters, Michaele and Buccio, for a catafalque in the middle of the church of St. Peter fifteen spans in length, twelve spans in width and six spans in height; furthermore, for a railing in the aisle, besides the catafalque to hold fifty torches and a hundred-and-fifty torchholders, also for benches for the mourners and a hundred prelates — everything for the price of a hundred-and-fifteen ducats, the ducat at ten carlines. He also arranged for a credence for the celebrant and that they should execute the catafalque and everything else during the whole of the following day.

Meanwhile the Pope, as has been told before, stood between the rails of the main altar and beside him there burned four torches. The decomposition and blackness of his face increased constantly so that he looked at eight o'clock, when I saw him, like the blackest cloth or the darkest negro, completely spotted, the nose swollen, the mouth quite large, the tongue swollen up, doubled so that it started out of his lips, the mouth open, in short so horrible that no one ever saw anything similar or declared to know of it.

In the evening after nine o'clock he was brought from there to the chapel of Santa Maria delle Febbri and deposited in the corner on the wall at the left of the altar by six porters who made jokes and allusions to the Pope all the while. The two carpenters had made the coffin too narrow and too short. They laid the mitre by his side, covered him with an old carpet and helped with their fists to fit him into the coffin.    All this without torches or any other illumination, without a priest or any person who took care of his body!    Thus told me Lord Chrispolit of St. Peter.

Hardness and falseness, madness and hate, rage, lustful
    desire,
Thirsty for blood and for gold, a sponge that can never
    be filled,
Alexander the sixth, here I lie; Roma rejoice thee
Free now at last; for my death was to mean new life
    for you.
Alexander the sixth has smothered the world in carnage,
Pius revives it again, worthy in name and in deed,
Alexander has sold the altars and crosses and Christum:
What he had gotten before, now he distributes again.

# APPENDIX

CHARLES VIII.— Philip de Comines, a contemporary of the French King, describes him as lacking in intelligence, and as being capricious and easily influenced, while Guiccardini, also a contemporary, had a much better opinion of him. Charles was short of stature and short-necked, with a parrot-like nose of enormous dimensions, a fiery birth-mark around his left eye, and twelve toes on his feet, hidden in splayed shoes, which set the fashion in foot-gear for the end of the fifteenth century in Italy.

INNOCENT VIII.— A good description of Innocent is contained in a report of the ambassador of Florence to his government: "He is a man," the ambassador writes, "of rather more than medium height, of fair culture, pleasant and kindly as a cardinal, more so than the dignity of a cardinal requires; he appears to be a man of peaceable disposition, but I doubt whether, in time, his office may not change his mind. He has an illegitimate son, who is now at Naples, a man of more than twenty years of age, and some married daughters, who themselves have sons; he has a brother and nephews besides, one of whom is a priest, a canon of St. Peter's, Messer Lorenzo by name, and it is thought that he will make him a cardinal at his first election of cardinals. Filippo di Nerone has a niece of his as his mistress, who was the wife of Stoldo Altovite, and when the Pontiff was a cardinal he held him in high esteem. He is naturally rather stout, fifty-three years of age, very prosperous, and an admirer of learned men."

Another contemporary, the historian Infessura, has this of him to say: " The vicar of the Pope in Rome and neighborhood, watchful of his flock as befits an honorable man, published an edict forbidding clergy as well as laics, whatever their position might be, to keep mistresses either openly or in secret. The penalty for so doing would be excommunication and confiscation of their benefices, for it was a practice which redounded to the discredit of priestly dignity and divine law. When the Pope heard this, he summoned the vicar and commanded him to annul the edict, saying that the practice was not forbidden. And indeed, such was the life led by the clergy that there was hardly one who did not keep a mistress. The number of harlots at that time living in Rome amounted to 6800, not counting those who practiced their nefarious trade under the cloak of concubinage and those who exercised their arts in secret."

Zizim (or Djem).— He was the younger son of Mahomet II and was defeated by his brother, Bajazet, when he attempted to drive him from the throne. He then took refuge with the knights at Rhodes. Sultan Bajazet used in turn both promises and threats to get the fugitive into his power. For greater safety Zizim went to France, where the Bishop of Aubusson undertook, on consideration of a pension of 45,000 ducats of gold, payable on the first of August in each year, to defray all the prince's expenses, and prevent his flight to re-open the struggle against his brother. In violation of his pledged word, the bishop treated the young prince not as his guest but as a prisoner. Several European princes insisted that Zizim should be delivered to them, especially Matthias of Hungary, who wished to make him serve his own designs against Bajazet II. The grand-master of the knights at Rhodes refused, and excused himself for his inability to deliver up Zizim, whom he was detaining in the Pope's name. Upon the representations of Innocent VIII, the King of France permitted the prince to be taken to Rome. Thereupon Turkish ambassadors came to Paris and made the most alluring offers to Charles VIII, if he would undertake to keep Zizim a prisoner. The king would not go back upon his word, and the Turkish ambassadors withdrew.

Zizim died in 1495 and the general opinion of contemporaries was that the prince had been poisoned. Money rewards for his death had indeed been offered repeatedly by Sultan Bajazet. It seems more likely, however, that the Turkish prince died a victim of the very irregular life he led and the five heavy meals he used to consume every day. It is very probable, though not proven, that Alexander VI received a bribe of 300,000 ducats for the return of Zizim's dead body, which was embalmed and shipped to Constantinople, where Bajazet received it with great pomp and a parade of mourning. An intercepted letter from the Sultan to the Pope mentioning this offer of money was delivered by Giovanni della Rovere to his brother, the Cardinal, who, detesting Alexander, promptly laid it before Charles VIII.

CPSIA information can be obtained at www.ICGtesting.com
Printed in the USA
LVOW110152291112

309225LV00014B/789/P

9 781171 701224